# SHUTTING OFF THE GAS TO GASLIGHTING

## RECLAIMING YOUR REALITY AND POWER IN A WORLD THAT TRIES TO DENY IT

JOHN WHEELER, LPCC-S

***Shutting Off the Gas to Gaslighting: Reclaiming Your Reality and Power in a World That Tries to Deny It***

Copyright © 2026 by John Wheeler, LPCC-S
ISBN (paperback): 978-1-63493-767-2
ISBN (eBook): 978-1-63493-768-9

All rights reserved. No part of this publication may be reproduced, stored in a retrieval system, or transmitted, in any form or by any means electronic, mechanical, photocopying, recording, or otherwise without prior written permission from the publisher.

The author and publisher of the book do not make any claim or guarantee for any physical, mental, emotional, spiritual, or financial result. All products, services and information provided by the author are for general education and entertainment purposes only. The information provided herein is in no way a substitute for medical advice. In the event you use any of the information contained in this book for yourself, the author and publisher assume no responsibility for your actions.

Published by Access Consciousness Publishing
www.acpublishing.com

*This book is dedicated to all the clients, class participants, inspirational friends and family whose stories helped to bring this book to life.*

# Table of Contents

# Introduction

***Reclaiming Your Reality and Power in a World That Tries to Deny It***

**Why This Book**

This isn't just another book on narcissism. It's not a handbook for diagnosing someone else. It's not a manual for making sure you're right or escaping "bad people." This book is about you. Your knowing, your nervous system, your energy, and your ability to choose what's true for you even when the world tries to convince you otherwise.

So, let's start here: *you are not crazy.*

If you've picked up this book, chances are you've been made to question your reality more times than you can count. You've been told you're overreacting. Too sensitive. That it never happened. You're imagining things. You twist things. You're just being dramatic. Maybe you've even heard the popular, "I'm only saying this because I love you." Sound familiar?

I wrote this because I've watched too many people – smart, aware, powerful people – start to question their own reality. Not because they were "weak," but because they were caught in something subtle, slippery, and socially sanctioned: *gaslighting.* The worst part is, with the insidious nature of gaslighting, you don't even notice that it's happening.

Gaslighting is one of the most confusing and subtle forms of psychological control. It doesn't always leave bruises, but it does leave you doubting yourself, your gut, your inner voice, and your sense of what's real. Over time, you start to hand over your power just to survive. And one day, you're completely unsure of who you are without that person's validation or their permission to choose.

By the time you're questioning your sanity, the damage has already begun. This book is here to help you *see it, name it, and shut off the gas* so you can come back to your own truth.

***It is a book about presence, about awareness – and more than anything, it's about choice.***

### What Gaslighting Is And What It Isn't

Let's get something straight: gaslighting is not just manipulation. It's not just someone being rude, dismissive, or having a bad opinion. It's not about disagreement or drama. Gaslighting is about psychological and energetic domination. It's not a one-time lie, it's a sustained strategy to make you doubt your own reality.

While manipulation might have a short-term goal (getting someone to say yes or do something), gaslighting's deeper intent is to make you abandon yourself. It's not about changing your mind. It's about replacing it. Your voice. Your view. *It doesn't just confuse you – it replaces your truth with theirs. Until theirs is the only one that feels real.*

Gaslighting works by making you feel wrong for asking questions, for naming things that feel off, or for reacting in ways that don't match the gaslighter's version of events. Over time, it strips away your clarity, until you rely on them to tell you what's true. And they'll be happy to provide that truth on their terms.

**Not a War on Gaslighters, But a Reclamation**

You might be expecting a takedown of toxic people. That's not what this book is.

This book is not about blaming, diagnosing, or launching a war against gaslighters. It's not about fixing the world or healing your past perfectly before you can move forward.

***This is not a war. This is a reclamation of you.***

Will we name the tactics? Yes. Will we explore how these patterns form? Yes. But the deeper work here is energetic. It's not just about what's being done to you, it's about how your energy gets hooked, and how you can choose to unplug from the game.

Because gaslighting only works if you *believe the lie.* When it echoes something you already fear. And most of us were trained to believe it – by our families, our culture, even ourselves.

The moment you stop feeding it with your reactions, your justifications, your emotional labor… the gas runs out.

That's what this book is about.

**The Therapeutic + Consciousness-Based Lens**

I didn't come to this topic casually. My background is both clinical and consciousness-based. I've worked for years as a licensed professional clinical counselor (mental health therapist) and as a life coach of many spritiual modalities. I've facilitated hundreds of people using using various tools and energetic processes, as well as clinical trauma-informed care. Outside of my clinical practice, I blend the psychological with the energetic because in real life, you are both.

I've walked with many individuals through the tangled mess of gaslighting and its effects, but I've also studied it through a different lens – the energetic one.

Gaslighting is not only mental and emotional. It is also energetic. By energetic, I mean there is often more happening than the words alone. It's the intensity behind the words, the tone, the look, the silence, the pressure in the room, and the way your body reacts before your mind can fully explain why. You may hear one thing being said, but feel something completely different landing in your system. That matters.

This is why gaslighting can be so disorienting. It doesn't just distort your thoughts or emotions, it can scramble your entire internal sense of reality. The gaslighter may deliver a false reality with so much force, certainty, charm, withdrawal, or emotional charge that it becomes easier to question yourself than to trust what you know.

When I talk about the energetic side of gaslighting in this book, I'm talking about that deeper layer: what your body, awareness, and nervous system are picking up, even when the words don't fully explain it. What is often labeled as "gaslighting" or "abuse" is actually a form of energetic control. They deliver an energy at you with so much intensity that it throws off your entire system. And the only way to lessen the intensity is to make it real. To capitulate to what they tell you is true. This is when the change begins.

You are a body with a nervous system. You are a being with awareness. And gaslighting affects both.

That's why this book can speak to both your mind and your energetic being. We'll explore how gaslighting shows up in somatic symptoms, emotional reactions, and spiritual confusion. And we'll also look at the deeper energetic anatomy of control, what it feels like in your body when someone is trying to dominate your reality, and what's possible when you reclaim your power to choose.

**The P.O.W.E.R. Process**

Throughout this book, you'll be introduced to a simple process you can use whenever gaslighting shows up in your life. It's not a complicated strategy or a script you have to memorize. It's simply a way to return to yourself in the moment. I call it ***P.O.W.E.R.***

Reclaiming your reality isn't about winning arguments or proving someone wrong. It's about staying connected to what you know even when someone else is trying to override it. The process looks like this:

**Pause (P):** Gaslighting works fastest when you react immediately. The first step is to pause and interrupt the reflex. Take a breath and give yourself a moment before responding.

**Observe (O):** Once you pause, you can notice what's actually happening. What was said? What did your body feel? What shifted in the moment? Observation separates the facts from the emotional noise.

**Witness the Pattern (W):** Gaslighting rarely happens only once. It follows patterns: phrases, behaviors, or emotional hooks that create confusion. When you recognize the pattern, clarity begins to replace doubt.

**Exit the Reaction (E):** Gaslighting feeds on reaction. The more you defend, explain, or chase understanding, the more energy the dynamic receives. Exiting the reaction allows the cycle to lose its fuel.

**Return to Yourself (R):** This is the heart of the process. Returning to yourself means reconnecting with your own awareness. What you sensed, what you noticed, and what you know to be true.

You'll see this process woven throughout the chapters

that follow. Sometimes it will be named directly, and other times it will appear through reflection exercises and practices. Each time you use it, you strengthen your ability to trust your own awareness again.

### If You've Ever Doubted Yourself

This book is for you if you've ever:

- Felt like you were "too sensitive" because you noticed things others ignored.
- Started explaining yourself more and more, only to feel less understood.
- Wondered if maybe you really were crazy.
- Found yourself looping on the same argument in your head for days.
- Spent more energy trying to prove your perspective than actually living your life.

If any of that sounds familiar, you're not broken – and you're not alone. You've just been gaslit. And your body knows it.

Here's what I *know*: you don't have to stay in the fog. You don't have to keep reacting. And you don't have to make yourself wrong to survive anymore.

This book isn't a magic bullet and it won't promise that

gaslighters will suddenly disappear from your life. (*Spoiler: they won't.*)

But it will give you the tools and awareness to make them irrelevant. To shut off the gas. To identify the hooks, clear the lies, and learn to trust your own knowing again – even if no one else validates it. The truth is, people may be able to support your knowing, but only you know what you know.

To take your voice back, not with a scream, but with an unshakable knowing that you are the source of your own reality.

***Once you reclaim your reality, no one can take it from you…ever!***

# PART I: THE ENERGY OF GASLIGHTING

# Chapter 1: What is Gaslighting, Really?

**Gaslighting vs. Manipulation**

Before we can talk about what gaslighting does to you, we need to clarify what it actually is – and what it is not. Most people use "manipulation" and "gaslighting" interchangeably, but your nervous system knows the difference even when your mind doesn't have the language for it.

Manipulation can exist in everyday life, sometimes even generatively. It can be used to create a new possibility, to influence a change, or to move something forward. For example: a therapist might manipulate a stuck point of view to help someone see from a different angle or a parent might manipulate a child into brushing their teeth. It's a nudge. An influence. You still remain you.

Gaslighting erases *you*. It's a slow, intentional override of your reality. It's not about changing your behavior, it's about confusing you so completely that you start to second-guess your every thought, choice, and action. It's about replacing *your* reality with *theirs* – until theirs is the only one that seems real. It's a total reorientation of your life that's centered around supplying something to them. You don't just lose the argument – you lose yourself.

While manipulation influences your choice, gaslighting removes it. The more it's repeated, the more it destabilizes your inner compass. You start questioning your own perceptions more than theirs. And when you do speak up, you're met with accusations: "You're overreacting. You always twist things. You're just being dramatic."

Gaslighting thrives when you stop believing yourself and start seeking their approval. That's what makes it so disorienting. It's not the lie – it's the erosion of your right to recognize the truth.

And here's the part no one tells you: it works because it's subtle.

Gaslighting doesn't usually show up with sirens and slaps. It starts in small ways. A dismissive laugh. A twisted retelling of something you said. A moment when you share your feelings and are told you're being ridiculous or too emotional. The first time, you brush it off. The second time, maybe you get irritated. By the third or fourth time, you start to wonder, *maybe I really am too sensitive…*

That's when the energy starts to land. And when it lands, it sticks. Then you buy it as something real and true, until it feels like an original thought. *Now it's yours!*

Over time, gaslighting can create a trauma loop – one where you're constantly seeking confirmation, craving clarity, and are stuck in an endless cycle of trying to prove your truth to someone who's never going to believe it. Or worse, someone who already knows it's true and is simply pretending it's not.

So, here's a simple definition I use:

*Gaslighting is the delivery of a false reality, with so much intensity that it becomes easier to believe it, than to keep questioning it.*

Why? Because the moment you push back, the gaslighter turns up the energy. They'll double down. Get louder. Or maybe even quieter, colder, withdrawn and stonelike. And suddenly, the easiest way to feel safe again is to back down.

But here's the truth: *gaslighting only works when you leave yourself.*

It only works when you stop trusting your awareness. When you hand over your power in favor of their stories and lies.

When you decide that staying in the relationship, the job, the friendship, the family dynamic is more important than staying connected to you.

***Manipulation*** includes choice. It may influence, persuade, or guide someone toward a desired outcome, often in a single instance.

***Gaslighting*** removes choice. It's about overriding the other person's sense of reality, so they stop choosing altogether.

| Manipulation | Gaslighting |
|---|---|
| Goal: influence your behavior or choice | Goal: control your perception of reality |
| Methods: guilt, pressure, persuasion, emotional leverage | Methods: denial, rewriting events, questioning your memory or sanity |
| Reaction: giving in to avoid conflict (if noticed at all) | Reaction: questioning your memory and perception, justifying and defending your choices |
| Your reality is usually still acknowledged and you still trust you. | Your reality is invalidated or erased and you doubt yourself. |

**The Energetic Anatomy: Control vs. Influence**

Gaslighting isn't just psychological – it's energetic. When

someone gaslights you, they're not just telling you a story. They're pushing an energy at you. It could be intense. Cold. Overwhelming. Sometimes it's wrapped in sweetness. Other times, it hits like a brick wall. Either way, your system feels it before your brain can name it.

Control is a command and demand for obedience. Control corners you into compliance. It's more about authority, having power over someone, rules and force, whereas influence leaves room for you to choose. When it comes to gaslighting, it always tips into control. It overrides, inserts and erases anything that doesn't match the other person's point of view or choice for you. Here's the key distinction: *Influence* is a collaborative approach to change and invites more awareness. You will feel the difference between control and influence.

The energetic anatomy of gaslighting feels like contraction. Your shoulders tighten. Your stomach drops. Your clarity vanishes. That's how you know it's not just a conversation – it's an energetic override.

One of the most disorienting tactics gaslighters use is sudden energetic withdrawal. The room goes cold. The conversation stops. They don't need to say, "You're wrong." They just make you feel like you are. It's energetic stonewalling. And it works because most of us were trained to doubt ourselves first.

When you collapse into that energy, you start spinning. You go into explanation, justification, or emotional reaction – all of which feed the cycle. The gaslighter regains control. You lose presence.

So what's the way out? Stillness. Presence. Expansion. If you stop matching their energy, their control has nothing to stick to. Silence becomes your power. Awareness becomes your clarity. You reclaim the ability to choose your response.

**Gaslighting is the Theft of Personal Reality**

At its core, gaslighting isn't just about power. It's about theft. The most damaging part of gaslighting isn't what they say – it's what you stop believing about yourself. It's the theft of your knowing. Your intuition. Your inner voice.

Gaslighting rewires you to default to someone else's version of reality. And it does so slowly. They don't take your clarity in one fell swoop. They chip away at it until you're afraid to speak, feel, or even think without double-checking.

This is why gaslighting is so effective. It teaches you to

outsource your truth. Not just in moments of conflict – but as a way of life. You learn to ask, "Is this okay?" instead of "Is this true for me?"

Over time, you may begin to say things like:

- "Maybe it is just me."
- "I'm probably too sensitive."
- "Maybe I'm remembering it wrong."

***Those aren't insights. They're symptoms of reality theft.***

The recovery begins when you stop asking for permission to know what you know. When you stop trying to convince the gaslighter and start choosing you. You stop supplying the gas, and without that fuel, their fire dies out.

# Chapter 2: Who Gaslights and Why?

Gaslighting doesn't always look like abuse. It often shows up as something far more subtle – something familiar, even loving at first glance. It can come from someone who raised you, someone who says they care about you, or someone who genuinely believes they're helping. That's what makes it so disorienting. You truly believe they have your best interest in mind.

Current society would have you believe that these types of people are evil, pointing to specific political or public figures known for the grandiose sense of self, but the truth is many people learn to gaslight. Perhaps they were raised by a parent who was a gaslighter so they've learned that gaslighting is the way to show you love and care about them. Maybe your evil ex wasn't purposely lying to you, but based on their own stories of abuse, they had learned to lie to preserve themselves.

I want to offer you something that most books won't:

***Every single person has gaslit someone.***

Gaslighting isn't just something *they do*. It's something *we all do*, especially when we're afraid. When we want to control a situation. When we're desperate to be seen, heard, validated, or safe. It's not always malicious. It's often learned. We gaslight ourselves (*more on this in Chapter 5*). We gaslight our kids. We gaslight our partners. We gaslight our bodies. And we usually don't even know we're doing it.

Gaslighting requires participation. Not conscious agreement, but energetic engagement. The moment you start to doubt yourself more than you doubt them, you begin to leave yourself behind, and the flames are lit.

In this chapter, we explore the different types of people who gaslight – not just those labeled as narcissists, but also the well-meaning, the wounded, and the ones repeating what they learned. We'll also look at the larger systems and patterns that condition people into gaslighting behaviors. And perhaps most importantly, we'll look at the energetic hook that makes their tactics land.

So, who actually gaslights? The typical answer would be narcissists, controllers, abusers, and people with personality disorders. They're often the worst and most common offenders, but the deeper truth is this: *People gaslight when they feel powerless but need to appear powerful.*

With this need in place, a gaslighter creates a false sense of superiority in order to make themselves feel strong, confident and invincible. They don't feel safe, so they need to dominate. They don't feel seen, so they need to invalidate you. They don't know what's true for them, so they need to rewrite your truth. Why? Because the more confused you are, the more confident and adequate they feel, and the easier you are to control.

Gaslighting becomes their coping mechanism. Their way of staying in charge, even when they're internally falling apart. This is what makes it so hard to catch. Many gaslighters appear to do things for the "right reasons," but in reality it always links back to their feeling of accomplishment. They might say all the right things, like "I only want what's best for you," while slowly robbing you of your inner knowing. Not through shouting or violence, but through carefully planted seeds of doubt. So subtle that you think it's your own voice.

### Narcissistic Types: Grandiose, Vulnerable, Communal, and Beyond

Let's begin with the most commonly named group:

*narcissists.* Narcissism exists on a spectrum, and not everyone who gaslights is a full-blown narcissist. But many gaslighters display narcissistic traits – especially when their identity depends on being seen a certain way. According to Dr. Ramani Durvasula, who is one of the leading experts in this field, there are eight identifiable types of narcissist: Grandiose, Covert/Vulnerable, Malignant, Communal, Neglectful, Benign, Entitled, and Generational/Cultural.

**Grandiose narcissists** tend to gaslight loudly. They dominate conversations, deny wrongdoing, and demand agreement. If you challenge them, they retaliate. Their gaslighting is overt and often aggressive: "You're crazy," "That never happened," or "You're twisting things again."

**Covert/Vulnerable narcissists** flip the script. They don't yell – they play the victim. They use guilt as a control tactic. If you express hurt, they respond with, "I can't believe you think that about me," or "You're so ungrateful." It's still gaslighting, just wrapped in fragility.

**Malignant narcissists** take the narcissistic need for control and mix it with cruelty, intimidation, or enjoyment of harm. Their gaslighting is often more punishing and deliberate. They may lie with confidence, provoke emotional reactions on purpose, and then use your pain as evidence that you are unstable. With this type, the goal is not just admiration or control, it can also be domination. They don't simply want to be right. They want you disoriented, diminished, and easier to overpower.

**Communal narcissists** hide in plain sight. They gaslight through virtue. These are the activists, teachers, or caregivers who say, "After everything I've done for you…" They use their goodness to make you question your badness, even when they're clearly crossing a line.

**Neglectful narcissists** gaslight through absence, indifference, and emotional starvation. They may not be dramatic or obviously controlling. Instead, they withhold attention, care, responsiveness, or acknowledgment, and then make you feel needy for wanting basic connection. Their message is often: "You're asking for too much," when in reality you're asking for something simple, human, and reasonable. This kind of gaslighting can be especially confusing because it often leaves no big scene to point to, only a slow erosion of your sense that your needs matter.

**Benign narcissists** can appear charming, harmless, or simply self-absorbed. They may not seem malicious, and they often don't fit people's stereotype of an abuser. But the impact can still be destabilizing. They consistently center themselves, minimize the experiences of others, and assume their perspective is the obvious one. If confronted, they may laugh things off, act confused, or dismiss your concerns as unnecessary drama. Their gaslighting often sounds casual, which can make you question yourself even more.

**Entitled narcissists** operate from the belief that the rules should bend for them. They expect special treatment, instant access, emotional compliance, or endless understanding. If you push back, they often respond as though you are the problem for not giving them what they deserve. Their gaslighting may sound like: "You're making this harder than it needs to be," or "If you really cared, you wouldn't question me." The underlying message is that their wants matter more than your reality.

**Generational/Cultural narcissists** show up less as one personality and more as a pattern of conditioning. It can live inside families, communities, institutions, or cultures where image matters more than truth, obedience matters more than awareness, and preserving the system matters more than protecting the individual. In these environments, gaslighting becomes normalized. You may hear things like: "That's just how they are," "Don't make trouble," or "We don't talk about things like that." The effect is the same: your reality is treated as the threat, while the distortion is protected.

Psychopathic or exploitative types use gaslighting as a strategy, not an accident. They manipulate reality on purpose to get something from you: power, access, control, or compliance. These types are often calm and calculated, which makes their gaslighting even harder to spot.

In every case, the goal is the same: create enough confusion that you question yourself and orient around them. That's the fuel they feed on.

**Cultural, Parental, and Systemic Gaslighting**

You don't become a gaslighter in a vacuum and it doesn't only happen between two individuals. These types of behaviors are woven into the systems we engage with on a daily basis. So much so, that search engines now confuse manipulation with gaslighting.

From early childhood, many of us are trained to override our inner knowing in favor of external authority. Think of how often children are told, "You're fine," when they're crying, or "Don't be dramatic," when they're scared. These may seem like harmless corrections, but they condition us to distrust our feelings and disconnect from the natural discernment we are born with. Perhaps in more neglectful or abusive environments a child may even become the scapegoat of the family and truly believe that everything that goes wrong is their fault because if the whole family believes it, it must be true. Right?

Discernment is the ability to sense what is true for you without immediately collapsing into someone else's version of reality. It's not judgment. It's not paranoia. And it's not about deciding who is "good" or "bad." Discernment is the inner capacity to notice: "Something feels off here, those words don't match the energy," or "What I'm being told doesn't line up with what I'm actually experiencing." It allows you to perceive clearly without needing to defend yourself instantly or make yourself wrong for noticing.

The problem is that many of us are raised not to trust discernment at all. We are taught to obey before we question, to be polite before we are honest, and to trust authority before we trust our own awareness. We're rewarded for compliance, not clarity. So when something feels off, instead of asking, "What do I know here?" we learn to ask, "What am I supposed to believe?" That is one of the earliest conditions that makes gaslighting possible: *the training to override discernment in order to belong, stay safe, or avoid conflict.* And for most people, that training begins at home.

In families, gaslighting can look like one parent always shifting blame or rewriting history to avoid responsibility. It can sound like, "That never happened," or "You always make things worse than they are." Over time, the child learns not to speak up, or worse, not to believe themselves at all.

Religious and cultural systems often gaslight too. They may teach that certain experiences are "just the devil testing you" or that your questions are "evidence of weak faith." In these spaces, curiosity and dissent are reframed as disloyalty, and you learn to mistrust your inner voice.

Gaslighting is also built into bureaucratic and educational systems. Think of schools or workplaces where reporting mistreatment is met with minimization, deflection, or punishment. These patterns teach people to doubt their reality in order to stay employed, enrolled, or accepted.

### Not Always Malicious: the "Loving" Gaslighter

Yes, many gaslighters display narcissistic traits. Some have full-blown narcissistic personality disorder, but not all of them. Narcissists tend to gaslight as a default strategy because to them, reality is always a performance. They need you to mirror what they want to see. If you don't, they'll either rage or retreat. Perhaps the hardest truth to swallow is this: *gaslighting isn't always malicious.* Sometimes, it's wrapped in concern. Sometimes, it looks like love.

You've probably heard things like:

- "I just worry about you."
- "You're too emotional to see clearly."
- "I'm only saying this because I love you."

Statements like these confuse care with control. The underlying message is, "You can't be trusted with your own reality so I'll define it for you." That's still gaslighting, even when it's done with a smile. They may not be trying to control you out of cruelty, they may be trying to feel safe, or right, or seen. You've got to ask yourself if their care is truly about you, or is it to make them feel better about themselves. What is the motivation for the behavior? That doesn't make the behavior okay, but it does explain why it's so pervasive.

| **Context** | **Gaslighting Phrase** | **Hidden Message** | **Likely Effect** |
|---|---|---|---|
| **Codependent Relationship** | "You wouldn't survive without my help." | *You are incapable without me.* | Dependency and reduced self-confidence. |
| **Work Environment** | "Everyone else understands this – why don't you?" | *You're the problem.* | Isolation and insecurity about competence. |

| **Spiritual Circles** | "Your ego is getting in the way of your growth." | *Your concerns are invalid.* | Feeling ashamed for questioning authority. |
|---|---|---|---|
| **Society/ Cultural Narratives** | "That didn't happen the way you think it did." | *Your experience of events is unreliable.* | Collective confusion about reality. |

### The Energetic Hook

What do you do with all this information? Here's the common thread in all of it: whether it's a narcissist, a parent, a partner, or a system, it only works if it hooks you and if you believe it. What makes it so powerful is when the lies echo something we already fear to be true about ourselves. "Maybe I am too much," "Maybe I really am the problem," or "Maybe I don't deserve better."

So, what if we move the conversation away from "Who is gaslighting me?" and consider "Why am I letting it work?" Not from blaming yourself and making yourself wrong, which only fans the flames, but from power. The power to recognize the lies you tell yourself and the ability to be totally aware of every thought, feeling, emotion and belief you have about yourself. That's why we don't just shut off the gas externally – we have to turn it off internally, too.

Gaslighting requires your *reaction*, your *uncertainty* and your *doubt* of what you already know.

So, before we go deep into strategies and responses, let's pause and ask:

- Who has gaslit you the most?
- What lie did you buy that made their version of reality feel more real than your own?
- What happens in your body when you believe yourself versus when you believe them?
- What pattern has repeated here, regardless of the promises, apologies, or explanations?
- What do you start questioning about yourself in this relationship that you don't question elsewhere?

What most gaslighters have in common is this: *they don't trust their own awareness so they project that distrust outward.* And if they can get you to question yourself the way they question themselves…they win.

But you don't have to play.

# Chapter 3: The Gas Supply: You

By now, you've started to see that gaslighting isn't just about what they say. It's about what happens *in you* when they say it.

A gaslighter can throw out a lie, a twist, a guilt trip, or a denial, but the part that really keeps the pattern going is your reaction. Your confusion. Your desperation to be understood. Your need for things to finally make sense. That's the gas.

This chapter is about the part no one wants to look at – not because you're to blame, but because this is where your power hides. Gaslighting needs fuel, and the uncomfortable truth is: *that fuel comes from you.* Your energy. Your attention. Your willingness to abandon yourself to stay connected to them.

Once you see how the gaslighter feeds off your reactions, your emotional triggers, and your desire to be chosen, you can start doing something radically different: *you can stop supplying the gas.*

### How Gaslighters Feed off Your Reactions

Gaslighters don't just want to win an argument, they want to secure their position as the authority on what's real. Your reactions are how they measure their success.

When you defend yourself, explain yourself, cry, beg, or shut down, something happens in the dynamic. You leave your center and move into their world. You start playing on their terms: proving, justifying, trying to make them see you. In that moment, your reality takes a back seat to their approval.

Most gaslighters are extremely skilled at reading reactions. They know when they've hit a nerve. If you start stammering, apologizing, or over-explaining, they know they've found the lever. If you get angry and raise your voice, they can now flip the narrative and call you unstable, irrational, or abusive. Either way, your reaction becomes their evidence.

Energetically, this looks like a hook. They throw out an intense energy – blame, superiority, hurt, disappointment – and your system scrambles to resolve it. You reach for logic, reassurance, or repair. Often, you reach for them. And that's exactly what they need: for you to orient around *them* instead of around your own *awareness*.

This is why some conversations with gaslighters always seem to end the same way. You might walk in clear and grounded, but by the time it's over you're spinning, apologizing, or wondering if you're the problem. The content of the conversation matters far less than the pattern: they provoke, you react, and then they position themselves as the calm, reasonable one.

Over time, this trains you to distrust your own responses. You begin to think, "If I get *this* upset, maybe they're right about me." But your reaction isn't proof that you're wrong. It's proof that your nervous system is overloaded by a dynamic that doesn't honor you.

The shift begins when you recognize that your reaction is part of the fuel. That doesn't mean you should suppress your feelings or force yourself to be neutral. It means you start choosing presence over performance. Instead of racing to defend or explain, you pause. You feel your feet. You notice your breath. You take a moment for yourself and quietly ask, "Do I actually believe what they're saying?"

When you stop rushing to manage their perception, something powerful happens: the gas has nothing to cling to. Your silence isn't compliance – it's clarity. Your lack of reaction isn't avoidance – it's refusal to supply more fuel.

## Emotional Triggers, Judgment, and the Lure of Validation

Most of us carry old stories about being too much, not enough, too sensitive, too needy, too dramatic, too intense. Those stories didn't start with the gaslighter. They started in families, schools, communities, and cultures that didn't know how to honor sensitivity, difference, or awareness. Gaslighters, whether consciously or unconsciously, aim right for those fault lines.

Gaslighting lands where there is already a wound.

If you already secretly fear you're too much, all they have to say is, "You're overreacting," and your body flinches. If you already worry you're not enough, a comment like, "No one else has a problem with this," can send you into shame. If you were raised to prioritize harmony over honesty, the accusation "You're causing drama" can shut you down instantly.

***Your own self-judgment becomes their best ally.***

Every place you've decided you're wrong, broken, or fundamentally flawed becomes an opening. Gaslighters don't have to create the wound, they just have to press on it. Then you do the rest. You spiral into self-blame, trying to fix yourself so the relationship can feel safe again.

Layered into this is the lure of validation. On some level, most of us are hoping that if we just explain ourselves well enough, if we stay patient and loving enough, if we are understanding enough, the gaslighter will finally say, "You're right. I see you. I get it." That fantasy is one of the strongest sources of gas.

You keep returning to the conversation not because anything changes, but because you are chasing that moment of being seen. You want the person who hurt you to also be the one who heals you. You want the person who distorted your reality to be the one who finally validates it.

Energetically, this looks like leaning out of yourself and into them. You reach for their recognition. You reach for their approval. You hand them the power to decide whether you're valid.

And here's the hard truth: if they needed to *invalidate you to feel powerful*, your vulnerability will not magically turn them into someone who can validate you. So what do you do instead?

You begin by noticing the trigger without judging it. "Wow,

that really stung. That comment hooked something old in me."

You acknowledge the story that got activated – "I'm too much. I'm the problem. I have to earn love" – and you gently name it as a story, not a fact.

Then, you ask, "If I weren't trying to get them to approve of me, what would I know here?" This doesn't make the pain vanish, but it shifts the focus. Instead of pouring your energy into getting *them* to see you, *you* start seeing you.

**The Myth of Needing Them to Choose You**

At the core of many gaslighting dynamics is one very powerful myth: *the belief that you need this person to choose you in order to be okay.*

You might not say it out loud, but it sounds like this on the inside:

- "If they finally understand me, I'll know I'm not crazy."
- "If they stay, it means I'm worth staying for."
- "If they apologize, then I'll know I wasn't the problem."

The gaslighter's power grows in proportion to how much you've made them the source of your worth, sanity, or belonging.

Gaslighters often sense this need and play directly into it. They may love-bomb you at the beginning, putting you on a pedestal and making you feel uniquely seen. Then, once you're invested, they begin to withdraw, criticize, or twist reality. The early idealization becomes the carrot you keep chasing: "If I can just get back to that version of us, everything will be okay."

In this setup, your entire nervous system orients around staying chosen. You tolerate behavior you never thought you would. You excuse things that deeply hurt you. You gaslight yourself to maintain the fantasy. The question quietly shifts from "Is this good for me?" to "What do I have to do so they don't leave?"

The myth here is that their choice creates your value, but your value doesn't fluctuate based on whether someone can see it. Your sanity doesn't disappear because someone calls you crazy. Your reality doesn't stop being real because someone refuses to validate it.

***What does change is how much of your own reality you're willing to abandon in order to keep theirs.***

Energetically, needing to be chosen pulls you out of

yourself. You leave your body, your awareness, your boundaries, and you hover anxiously in their world – reading every tone, every pause, every message, every silence for clues about where you stand.

The turning point comes when you ask a different question: "What if I chose me, even if they never do?"

This isn't about slamming a door or cutting someone off to prove a point (*though sometimes leaving is the kindest choice*). It's about reclaiming the basic truth that your reality, your body, and your knowing belong to you – *NOT* to whoever happens to be in front of you.

When you no longer need them to choose you, their tactics lose leverage. They can still withdraw approval, twist stories, or refuse accountability, but it no longer defines you. You might still feel sad, disappointed, or angry. But you won't be for sale.

### End-of-Chapter Exercise: Tracking Your Gas Supply

Take a few minutes with a journal and explore the following:

1. **Pause.** Think of a recent interaction where you left feeling confused, small, or wrong. Before analyzing

it, take a breath and slow the moment down. In your journal, write what happened as clearly as you can remember it. Focus on the actual sequence of events – what was said, what you said in response, and what shifted in the conversation.

2. **Observe.** Now reread what you wrote and notice the moments where you reacted. Where did you defend yourself, explain your intentions, shut down, or try to chase reassurance? Circle those moments. These are often the places where the conversation gained energy and where you may have unknowingly supplied gas to the dynamic.

3. **Witness the Pattern.** As you look again at the interaction, underline any phrases, thoughts, or feelings that touched something deeper inside you. These may sound like familiar inner messages such as "I'm too much," "It's my fault," or "I'm not enough." These reactions often reveal old triggers or patterns that the moment activated.

4. **Exit the Reaction.** Notice where in the interaction you felt pulled to keep explaining, defending, or proving your perspective. Reflect on where you might have been hoping to be chosen, validated, or rescued.

These are the places where the reaction tends to keep the cycle going.

5. **Return to Yourself.** "Finally, ask yourself: If I had not needed their approval in that moment, what would I have known? What would I have trusted about my own perception? What might I have chosen instead?" Let your answer come honestly, without forcing it.

You don't have to change everything at once. Simply seeing where your gas is going is the beginning of shutting off the supply.

***Awareness is the first step in reclaiming your reality.***

# PART II: SEEING THROUGH THE SMOKE

# Chapter 4: The Seductive Cycle of Emotional Control

If gaslighting is the theft of your reality, love bombing, hoovering, stonewalling, narcissistic rage and flying monkeys are often the delivery system.

These tactics don't usually show up as obvious abuse at first. They show up as intensity, attention, or as "finally, someone sees me." They create a cycle that feels like *connection*, but is actually *emotional control.* You get swept into something that feels big, special, and undeniable until the ground starts to move under your feet.

This chapter is about that cycle: the big highs, the crushing lows, the sudden walls of silence, the explosive eruptions that seem to come out of nowhere, and the people who get recruited into the gaslighter's story. We'll look at how these patterns play out in romantic relationships, families, friendships, and groups, and most importantly, how to recognize them before you get pulled back in again.

These patterns can sound similar because they are. Love bombing, hoovering, stonewalling, narcissistic rage, and flying monkeys are not separate, random tactics. They are variations of the same cycle of emotional control. Each one may look different on the surface, but they all serve the same function: to destabilize your reality, pull you back into self-doubt, and keep you engaged with the gaslighter's version of truth. That's why this chapter circles similar emotional territory more than once, because the cycle itself does. It repeats, shifts form, and comes back around, until you begin to see what's different. It is often one pattern wearing different faces.

**Love Bombing: The Illusion of Deep Connection**

Gaslighters rarely start with cruelty. They start with seduction.

Not necessarily sexual seduction (*though that happens too*), but energetic seduction. They show up as everything you've been asking for: attentive, available, understanding, "different" from everyone else. They listen deeply. They mirror your values. They tell you they've never met anyone like you.

This is the front end of love bombing.

Love bombing is the phase where you're flooded with

affection, praise, attention, or support. It can come in the form of constant messages, grand gestures, rapid intimacy, or sudden declarations of a lifelong bond. They may say things such as, "I've never connected like this with anyone. You're my soulmate. We're family now."

In a family or group, it might sound like, "You're the only one who really understands," or "You're my favorite," or "You're not like the others."

Energetically, love bombing feels expansive and intoxicating. Your body relaxes. Your nervous system goes, "Finally." You let all of your barriers and discernments go in order to show up totally vulnerable as yourself under the guise that they finaly understand you. Maybe you've spent a lifetime feeling unseen, like too much, or like you were never enough. Suddenly someone is pouring energy on all the parts of you that have been starving. It's not wrong to enjoy that. The problem is what comes next.

Because love bombing isn't just about *connection*, it's about *creating a contrast.*

Once you've experienced that high level of attention and affirmation, it becomes the reference point. So when they begin to pull away, criticize, or rewrite reality, you don't just feel confused. You feel withdrawal. You feel loss. You start working and changing your actions to "get back" to the version of them who was so generous, so understanding, so in love with you. It's like a drug that you seek and you have to completely modify parts and pieces of yourself to maintain that deep connection, or not create upset in your relationship. This becomes the fuel to avoid conflict, challenge and opposition to what the gaslighter sets as true.

**Hoovering: Pulling You Back In**

Hoovering is the next phase of this cycle. Named after a vacuum cleaner, it describes what happens when you start to pull away, or when the gaslighter senses they're losing control. Suddenly they reappear with apologies, tears, explanations, or new promises. "I'll go to therapy. I've never felt this way about anyone. I know I messed up, but I can change." They might reference the early days: "Remember how good it was between us? We can have that again."

What they're really doing is reopening the energetic loop they created with love bombing. They give you just enough of that *old* version of them to hook you back in. You feel relief: "There they are. I knew I wasn't crazy." You might even take their return as proof that you matter to them. But notice something: *it rarely comes with consistent action or follow through.*

Their return comes as a perfect fantasy and a manipulation – they can be who you believe they are, but you never see them as they actually are. There's a lot of energy, a big dream, and emotional grand gestures. And then, within days or weeks, the gaslighting resumes. You go back to supplying the gaslighter with fuel and the cycle starts again.

**Stonewalling: Controlling You Through Silence**

Stonewalling is another key tactic in this cycle. Where hoovering pulls you back in with words and emotion, stonewalling controls you through absence.

The gaslighter shuts down, goes silent, withholds affection, eye contact, or response. They may ignore your messages, walk away mid-conversation, give you the cold shoulder for days, or sit in icy silence while insisting "nothing is wrong." It's an ultimate form of control because how can you change something if you don't have any information. The truth is, they can't offer you the information because you'll see the insidious nature of the cycle. It's designed to keep you guessing and always in doubt of what's going to happen.

Energetically, stonewalling feels like hitting a wall you

can't see. Your nervous system scrambles to make sense of the sudden cold. You may find yourself begging for engagement, apologizing just to get them to speak, or replaying everything you said to figure out what you did wrong. You begin to feel punished for something you did without knowing what you did.

It adds a level of guilt, plays on inner narratives of shame, plays on our fears of loss and abandonment. That frantic self-searching is the fuel. The more you chase, the more power the stonewalling has.

***You start to learn: connection is conditional, and silence is punishment.***

### Narcissistic Rage: Punishment for Disrupting the Fantasy

If love bombing is the seduction, hoovering is the pull back in, and stonewalling is the wall of silence, narcissistic rage is often the punishment for disrupting the gaslighter's version of reality.

Narcissistic rage doesn't always look like screaming, though sometimes it does. It can be explosive and obvious – yelling, insults, threats, slamming doors, dramatic accusations. But it can also be cold, sharp, and controlled. It may sound like contempt, cruel mockery, character assassination, or a sudden flood of blame meant to put you back in your place.

What triggers it? Usually some form of injury to the gaslighter's self-image. You question them. You set a boundary. You stop complying. You notice the pattern. You leave. You refuse to accept their version of reality. In that moment, your awareness becomes a threat, not just to their control, but to the identity they're desperately trying to protect.

Energetically, narcissistic rage can feel like being hit by a wave. The intensity rises so quickly that your body may go into instant survival mode. You freeze. You appease. You shut down. You try to soothe them, explain yourself, or backtrack just to make it stop. And that is exactly why rage becomes such an effective control tactic. It teaches you that telling the truth, having a boundary, or simply being your own person comes with punishment.

This is important to understand: narcissistic rage is not proof that *you did something wrong.* It is often proof that *you touched something true.*

That doesn't mean every angry person is narcissistic, and it doesn't mean conflict itself is abuse. Healthy people can get angry. Healthy people can lose their cool.

The difference is what happens next. In a conscious relationship, anger can lead to reflection, repair, and accountability. In a gaslighting dynamic, rage is used to overpower, intimidate, or silence. It becomes another way of saying "My version of reality wins."

After narcissistic rage, many people find themselves doubting their own memory of the event. The gaslighter may later minimize it, deny it, blame you for causing it, or act as though it never happened. This creates an especially destabilizing loop: *first the explosion, then the rewriting.* First the punishment, then the denial. Over time, you may become so focused on avoiding the rage that you start abandoning yourself before they even have to push.

That anticipation is part of the control.

Recognizing narcissistic rage for what it is can be deeply liberating. It helps you stop interpreting their intensity as evidence of your guilt. It reminds you that someone else's eruption is not the same thing as your wrongdoing. And it gives you information: if your honesty, boundaries, or independence reliably trigger punishment, then the relationship is not built on mutual respect. It is built on control.

## Flying Monkeys: The Reinforcement Squad

Flying monkeys are often the final piece of this control pattern. Once the gaslighter has spun a story about you being unstable, ungrateful, selfish, or "the problem," they may recruit others to carry that story. These "flying monkeys" (*a reference to the minions in The Wizard of Oz*) can be family members, friends, coworkers, or members of a spiritual or social group.

They might say things like:

- "They're really trying, you know. Maybe you could be more understanding."
- "You know how sensitive you are. I'm sure they didn't mean it that way."
- "You're blowing this out of proportion. They said they were sorry."
- "I've talked to them. This all sounds like a big misunderstanding."

Sometimes flying monkeys are actively manipulative. Other times, they're just deeply invested in maintaining the gaslighter's image or the stability of the group. They may genuinely think they're helping by encouraging you to "let it go" or "not make waves." But the role they serve, whether cognitively or not, is the same: *to redirect your doubt back at you.*

This tactic is unique in a way because leaving a narcissistic or gaslighting relationship doesn't always mean the flying monkeys disappear. Often, their role actually intensifies once you step away. Flying monkeys serving in this role are often the least aware and are effective because they genuinely do care for you.

Instead of saying, "Give them another chance," they may become the messengers of the gaslighter's narrative:

- "They're really worried about you. They said you're not doing well since the breakup."
- "They told us they did everything they could. You just wouldn't meet them halfway."
- "We just want you to see your part in this. You know how you can be."

Behind the scenes, the gaslighter may be triangulating by telling your family, mutual friends, or community that you're the unstable one, you're "crazy," "ungrateful," or "too sensitive," so that by the time you leave, there's already a story in place about who you are and why the relationship ended.

Energetically, this keeps you on trial long after you've walked away. You might notice:

- People pulling away or going cold without explanation.
- Relatives or friends suddenly "taking sides."
- Concerned messages that sound caring on the surface but are actually repeating the gaslighter's point of view.

The goal is the same as when you were still in the relationship: to make their version of reality more real than yours, and to pressure you through guilt, shame, or "concern" into doubting your own awareness and possibly going back.

This is where your boundaries and presence matter most. You don't have to defend yourself against every rumor. You don't have to explain your side to people who are already committed to the gaslighter's story. You get to choose:

- Who has access to you.
- Who gets details about your life.
- Who has earned the right to hear your reality.

You're not obligated to participate in conversations that exist only to pull you back into the old role you've just left.

Together, love bombing, hoovering, stonewalling, narcissistic rage, and flying monkeys create a loop:

idealization, confusion, punishment, silence, partial repair, and pressure to stay. It's not random. It's a system designed to keep your energy feeding the dynamic, to keep you fanning the flames.

Sometimes the clearest way to understand this cycle is to watch how it actually plays out in someone's life.

### Client Case Scenario: When "Finally" Turns into Fog

When Ava met Daniel, it felt like relief. He seemed deeply attentive, emotionally available, and unusually interested in who she really was. He remembered small details, mirrored her values, and said things like, "I've never connected like this with anyone," and "You're the only one who really understands me." After years of feeling unseen in relationships, Ava felt chosen. Her body softened. Her guard came down. She thought, Finally. Someone gets me. (*This was the beginning of the seduction.*)

At first, Daniel's attention felt like love. Then it became the standard Ava kept trying to get back to. When his tone changed, when he became more critical, or when he dismissed her concerns with, "You're overthinking it," or "That's not what happened," she didn't immediately see it as control. She saw it as something she needed to fix. She started editing herself, softening her words, and working harder to avoid upsetting him. She kept reaching for the version of him from the beginning.

When Ava tried to talk about what felt off, Daniel often shut down completely. He'd go cold, stop responding, or insist "nothing is wrong" while clearly punishing her with silence. Ava would replay every conversation, wondering what she had done. She apologized just to restore connection. Over time, she started to believe that their connection was conditional.

When Ava finally had the courage to address what she was noticing and how she was feeling, Daniel exploded. He accused her of being manipulative, dramatic, and impossible to please. His rage felt wildly disproportionate to what she had actually said. Ava froze, then backtracked, then tried to calm him down. By the next day, he acted as if nothing had happened. When she brought it up, he told her she was exaggerating and remembering it wrong.

When Ava finally pulled away, Daniel reappeared with apologies, tears, and promises. He said he would change. He reminded her of how good things were in the beginning. He gave her just enough warmth and hope to make her doubt herself and reopen the door. For a moment, she felt relief: There he is. I knew I wasn't crazy. But within days, the criticism and confusion returned.

After the breakup, mutual friends started reaching out. Some told her Daniel was "really worried" about her. Others suggested it was all just a misunderstanding. A few hinted that she was being too sensitive. Without realizing it, they were reinforcing his narrative and pulling her back into self-doubt.

What finally changed was not Daniel. It was Ava's willingness to trust what the relationship actually felt like in her body. She stopped trying to get back to the fantasy version of him. She stopped arguing for her reality with people committed to misunderstanding it. She started asking different questions: What do I know here? What is this pattern showing me?

That was the beginning of the end of the cycle.

### Spotting Toxic Cycles in Romantic, Family, and Group Dynamics

These tactics don't only show up in romantic relationships. They appear in families, friendships, workplaces, and spiritual communities. The details may change, but the energetic structure is remarkably similar.

### Romantic Relationships

In romantic relationships, love bombing can look like:

- Rapid declarations of love or commitment, typically after a fight, arguement or disagreement.
- Intense communication early on (*constant texts, calls, future plans*) only to decrease after you make it official.
- Putting you on a pedestal and calling you "the only one who understands."

Then later:

- Subtle criticism or blame.
- Denying things they clearly said or did.
- Using your reactions as proof that you're the unstable one.
- Disappearing or withdrawing, only to reappear when you pull away or give in.
- Long stretches of cold silence, shutdown, or refusal to engage.

### Family Dynamics

In families, love bombing might show up as being the "golden child" one moment and the scapegoat the next. A parent or caregiver showers you with affection, brags about you to others, or makes you feel like you're their favorite until you express a boundary or disagree. Suddenly you're "ungrateful," "selfish," or "too sensitive." They may then triangulate with siblings, relatives, or other adults, turning them into flying monkeys who pressure you to fall back in line. "Why can't you be more like your brother? You take things too seriously!"

Stonewalling in families can look like being frozen out. Parents or relatives refusing to speak to you, not responding to calls or messages, or acting as though you're invisible at gatherings. The message is clear: *conform or lose connection.*

**Groups, Workplaces, and Spiritual Communities**

In group or community dynamics like workplaces, clubs, or spiritual circles, love bombing can look like being fast-tracked, singled out, or invited into the "inner circle." You might be told you're special, chosen, or more advanced than the others, which feels flattering, especially if you've longed for recognition.

But if you question the leader, refuse an expectation, or point out an inconsistency, the tone can change quickly. Now you're "negative," "not a team player," or "in your ego."

Stonewalling in groups might look like being left off emails, excluded from meetings, or suddenly treated as if you don't exist. No one explains why, you just feel the door close.

People you thought were peers may suddenly distance themselves or try to convince you to "get back on board." Those are flying monkeys at work.

What all of these cycles share is *instability*. You're never quite sure where you stand. Safety and connection feel conditional.

You might notice:

- You're walking on eggshells, trying not to "mess up" the good moments.
- You're constantly replaying conversations, trying to figure out what you did wrong.
- You feel a drop in your body when their tone shifts, a message goes unanswered, or others start treating you differently.
- You keep hoping the "old" version of them or the group will come back if you can just fix whatever you supposedly did.

These are signs you're in a toxic cycle, not just a difficult relationship or rough patch. The pattern isn't moving toward more honesty and mutual respect. It's moving toward more control. And remember: it's not your job to diagnose the gaslighter or convince the flying monkeys.

Your power lies in recognizing what's happening and choosing how you will or will not participate.

**End-of-Chapter Exercise: Mapping the Cycle**

Take some time with a journal and explore the following questions:

1. **Pause.** Think of a relationship – past or present – where you experienced both intense closeness and deep invalidation. Take a moment to slow down and bring the relationship clearly to mind. In your journal, write down specific examples of the "highs," such as moments of affection, attention, or love bombing, alongside the "lows," including gaslighting, withdrawal, criticism, or sudden emotional distance.

2. **Observe.** As you review what you wrote, notice any moments when the other person softened, reappeared, or became affectionate right as you were beginning to pull away. Write about what they said or did in those moments and how it affected your decision to stay, reconnect, or give the relationship another chance.

3. **Witness the Pattern.** Now reflect on times when the person shut down, went cold, or refused to engage with you. Write about how you responded to that stonewalling and what you began to believe about

yourself during those moments. Notice whether those reactions echo familiar patterns you have experienced in other relationships.

4. **Exit the Reaction.** Consider whether other people reinforced the version of events that kept the dynamic in place. Were there friends, family members, or colleagues who supported their perspective, subtly or directly? Write down what was said and how it affected your trust in your own perception. Notice where you may have felt pressure to explain, defend, or prove yourself.

5. **Return to Yourself.** Now ask yourself: "If I stopped chasing the high of being chosen, what would I know about this relationship? What might it feel like to create relationships where love doesn't have to be earned through intensity, loyalty, or self-abandonment?" Sit with whatever awareness arises, even if it doesn't match what you once hoped was true.

Remember: seeing the cycle is not about blaming yourself for being in it. It's about reclaiming your capacity to choose something different.

***Every moment you choose awareness over their lies, you shut off a little more of the gas.***

# Chapter 5: Self-Gaslighting

If gaslighting is the process of someone else convincing you to doubt your reality, self-gaslighting is what happens after you've lived in that distortion long enough that you begin doing it to yourself.

You no longer need the gaslighter in the room to question your feelings, minimize your pain, or rewrite your own story. You've internalized their voice. Their judgments now sound like your thoughts. Their confusion feels like your truth.

This chapter is about that inner echo. The part of you that learned to doubt yourself in order to stay safe, loved, or acceptable. We'll explore how the voices of others get installed inside your head, what happens when your own identity gets reduced to reflection, and how you can begin choosing what's true for you again, even after years of abandoning yourself.

## How We Internalize the Voices of Others

Self-gaslighting doesn't appear out of nowhere. It's learned.

From an early age, most of us are told some version of:

- "You're fine" when our body says we're not.
- "That didn't hurt" when it clearly did.
- "Don't be dramatic" when we express strong emotion.
- "Be nice" when our instincts say, "This isn't safe."

Over time, these messages train us to override our own signals. We begin to treat our perceptions as suspicious and other people's interpretations as authoritative.

When you're repeatedly gaslit by someone close to you – a parent, partner, boss, friend, teacher – this process intensifies. Every time they deny what you saw, felt, or heard, you're faced with an impossible choice: either believe yourself and risk losing them, or believe them and lose yourself.

For many people, especially children, the body makes the most survival-based choice: *abandon self, attach to other.*

Eventually, you don't need them there to continue the pattern. Their voice has become internalized.

- You start to say, "Maybe I'm overreacting" before anyone else has a chance to.
- You instinctively downplay your own discomfort: "It's not that big of a deal." Or "It's not that serious."
- You rewrite your memory to match what you think someone else would prefer: "Maybe I remembered it wrong."

This is self-gaslighting: using the same tactics that were used on you – denial, minimization, blame – against your own awareness.

Energetically, it feels like turning away from yourself in the moment you most need you. Your body tenses, your chest tightens, your mind starts scrambling for why you're wrong.

Instead of offering yourself care or curiosity, you offer yourself criticism and doubt. Rather than practicing self-compassion and reflection, you practice self-deprication and judgment.

The problem with self-gaslighting is that it keeps the original dynamic alive long after the external gaslighter is gone. You may physically leave the relationship, change jobs, move cities, or set boundaries with family, and still find yourself questioning every feeling, apologizing for existing, or needing permission to know what you know.

The first step in changing this isn't to "stop doing it" overnight. It's to *notice* it. Not as proof that you're broken, but as evidence of how adaptive and loyal you've been. You were willing to turn against yourself in order to stay connected to something or someone you believed in. That might not be kind to you, but it makes sense given what you learned.

**Echoism: The Loss of Voice and Identity**

There's a term sometimes used in discussions about narcissistic dynamics: *echoism*. It comes from the myth of Echo and Narcissus (*see the resources for the full myth*). In Ovid's telling, Echo is a mountain nymph who once had a full voice of her own, but after angering Hera, she is cursed so that she can no longer speak freely and can only repeat the last words spoken to her. Then she falls in love with Narcissus, a beautiful young man who rejects every admirer and is incapable of returning love. Echo can't fully express herself, can't initiate her own words, and can only reflect back what is given to her. After Narcissus rejects her, she fades until only her voice remains. Later, Narcissus is punished for his coldness by falling in love with his own reflection, becoming consumed with his own image rather than capable of real relationship.

The connection between them is what makes the myth so powerful here. Echo loses herself by becoming all response and no self, while Narcissus is so fixated on himself that no one else can fully exist in the relationship. That dynamic mirrors what happens in many gaslighting and narcissistic systems: one person takes up all the emotional space, and the other slowly disappears trying to maintain connection. Echo becomes a voice without a center; Narcissus becomes a self with no real capacity for considering others. Together, they tell the story of what happens when one person can only reflect and the other can only take.

In a gaslighting dynamic, especially with highly self-focused or narcissistic people, you may learn to function like Echo. Your role becomes more about reflecting the needs, moods, and narratives of the other person, while abondoning your own. Your own thoughts, desires, and preferences shrink or disappear entirely.

Echoism isn't a diagnosis. It's a pattern of *self-erasure.*

It looks like:

- Waiting to see how someone else feels before you decide how you feel.
- Adopting other people's opinions to avoid

conflict.
- Describing yourself mostly in relation to others ("I'm a good partner. I'm a supportive friend. I'm a hard worker") rather than as a being with an inner life.
- Feeling uncomfortable or even guilty when attention is on you in a genuine way.

When you've spent years, or even decades, in relationship with someone who dominates the emotional space, your system may conclude that the safest place for you is in the background. You become the echo to their narrative.

Layer self-gaslighting on top of that, and you get an even more painful combo: not only do you suppress your voice, but when it does try to appear, you immediately doubt or attack it. You think, "Who am I to feel this way?" or "I'm probably making this up."

Energetically, echoism feels like being half a step behind yourself. You sense something, but you look outward before letting it land inward. You check the room, the relationship, the group, the leader, the partner, or the family to see what's allowed. Only then do you tentatively shape your response and pretend it was your choice.

Take someone like Marissa. She's in a group setting with

friends trying to decide where to go for dinner. At first, she notices that she feels tired and wants somewhere quiet. But before she says anything, she scans the room. One friend seems excited, another is already leaning toward the louder place, and someone jokes that the quieter option would be "boring." Almost instantly, Marissa disconnects from her first awareness and says, "I'm good with whatever everyone else wants." Later, when she's overwhelmed, overstimulated, and irritated, she tells herself she has no right to feel that way because no one forced her to agree. But the truth is, she never really included herself in the choice to begin with.

This same pattern can show up in much bigger ways. A person senses discomfort in a relationship, notices that something feels off, and then immediately starts explaining it away: "Maybe I'm too sensitive. Maybe I'm being unfair. Maybe I just need to be easier to be with." Instead of letting their awareness deepen, they reflect back the needs, moods, and preferences of the other person until they can no longer tell the difference between accommodation and truth. That is the quiet pain of echoism: not simply losing your voice, but losing access to the moment where it would have begun.

However, the loss of voice and identity isn't a character

flaw. It's the aftermath of living in environments where having a clear "you" was punished, shamed, or ignored.

The good news? If echoism is learned, it can be unlearned. Your voice is not gone, it's buried. Your identity is not missing, it's covered up by layers of survival strategies.

### Choosing What's True for You Again

Recovering from self-gaslighting and echoism isn't about becoming loud, confrontational, or "never doubting yourself again." It's about rebuilding an intimate, trusting relationship with *your own awareness*.

That starts with very small, very simple choices:

- Noticing when you dismiss your first instinct.
- Catching yourself when you say, "I'm probably overreacting," and pausing instead of automatically believing it.
- Asking, "What do I know here?" before asking, "What would they say about this?"
- Observing the beliefs you have about yourself and asking how you've come to that conclusion.

At first, choosing what's true for you might feel risky. Your body remembers times when truth led to conflict, abandonment, or attack. So it's important to move gently.

You don't need to announce your truth to everyone around you. You don't need to debate or convince. This part of the journey is completely about you, between you and for you.

***There is never a reason to justify any of your choices.***

You might start by honoring small preferences:

- Admitting to yourself that you don't like something you've pretended to enjoy.
- Letting yourself rest when your body is tired instead of pushing through to meet someone else's expectation.
- Saying no to a minor request and noticing that the world doesn't end.

Each of these is a way of saying: "My reality matters."

As you do this, the inner gaslighter will likely protest. You may hear thoughts like: "You're selfish," "You're being difficult," or "You're going to lose people." When that happens, instead of arguing with those thoughts, you can recognize them as echoes. They are old recordings, not present-tense truths.

You can respond internally with something like: "Thank you for trying to keep me safe, but I'm choosing differently now." This acknowledges the protective function those patterns once had, without continuing to let them run the show. After all, they are the adaptations you made to survive the moment. Now what choices can you make?

Choosing what's true for you doesn't mean you'll never make mistakes or change your mind. It means you stop abandoning yourself as your default setting. It means you give yourself permission to have your own experience even if no one else understands it or agrees with it.

### End-of-Chapter Exercise: Listening for Your Own Voice

Set aside some quiet time with your journal and explore the following prompts:

1. **Pause.** Take a moment to slow down and listen to the inner dialogue that runs quietly in the background of your thoughts. In your journal, write down three "voices" that sound critical, dismissive, or shaming. For each one, ask yourself: "Who does this sound like?" You may notice echoes of parents, partners, teachers, authority figures, or cultural messages you absorbed over time.

2. **Observe.** Now think of a recent moment when you overrode your own feeling, need, or perception. Write about what happened and what you initially sensed in

the first few seconds before you talked yourself out of it. What did your body or intuition register before the inner voices began explaining it away?

3. **Witness the Pattern.** Reflect on one area of your life where you feel particularly voiceless or undefined. This could be in relationships, work, creativity, spirituality, or another part of your world. As you write, ask yourself: "If I weren't trying to be the 'good,' agreeable, or easy one here, what would I actually choose?" Allow your answer to come without editing or correcting yourself.

4. **Exit the Reaction.** For the next week, choose one small daily action that affirms your own knowing. It might be setting a tiny boundary, honoring a preference, giving yourself a moment of rest, or telling the truth in your journal. Write down the action you will practice and notice where you would normally override yourself but instead choose something different.

5. **Return to Yourself.** Place a hand somewhere on your body – your heart, chest or belly – and take a slow breath. In your journal, or out loud if you can, say: "My reality matters. My voice matters. I am

learning to choose me again." As you do, notice any sensations or emotions that arise. Let whatever you feel be present without judging it or trying to change it.

You don't have to silence the inner gaslighter overnight. You just have to stop letting it be the only voice you trust.

***Every time you choose to listen to yourself, not the echoes, you are shutting off the gas and becoming more of you.***

# Chapter 6: Gaslighting in the Wild

So far, we've been looking at gaslighting up close and personal: the partner, the parent, the friend, the boss. But gaslighting doesn't just happen in individual relationships. It's woven into the larger systems and spaces we move through every day.

Workplaces, religious institutions, political movements, and media all have the power to shape what we see as real. When those systems are healthy, they can offer support, structure, and shared meaning. When they're unhealthy or invested in control, they can distort reality on a massive scale.

This chapter is about gaslighting in the wild: the ways culture, institutions, and public figures can make you question your awareness, doubt your experience, and override your inner knowing.

We'll look at how this shows up in work, religion, politics, and media; how public narratives can become weapons; and what to do when reality itself starts to feel like a moving target.

### Work, Religion, Politics, and Media

Gaslighting in systems often feels different from gaslighting in intimate relationships, but the mechanics are similar. There is still a dominant narrative. There is still a pressure to conform. There is still a cost to holding on to what you know is true.

In the workplace, gaslighting can look like:

- Being told a problem doesn't exist when you're living with it every day.
- Reporting unethical behavior and being told you're "misinterpreting" or "overreacting."
- Having your contributions minimized or credited to someone else.
- Being labeled "negative" or "not a team player" when you name real issues.

Over time, you may start to think, "Maybe it's just me. Maybe I'm the difficult one." Your body, however, will often tell a different story – stress, anxiety, dread – before work, a sense of collapse every time you're asked to "get on board" with something that feels off.

In religious or spiritual spaces, gaslighting often comes dressed as guidance or care. You might hear:

- "That's just your ego talking."
- "You're out of alignment if you question this."
- "If you had more faith, or believed enough, you wouldn't feel that way."
- "You're creating this with your negativity."

Here, your natural questions and intuitive red flags get reframed as spiritual failure. You're not discerning, you're disloyal. You're not aware, you're attacking the group. This is especially confusing when the language being used includes consciousness, healing, or love.

In politics, gaslighting often takes the form of rewriting history or denying obvious harm. Leaders or parties may insist something is "fake news" even when there is clear evidence, or they may minimize consequences that are visibly impacting people's lives. Some may even create a problem, then present a solution without ever acknowledging they created the problem in the first place.

You might notice yourself thinking "But I see what's happening… why are they saying the opposite?" That tension, between what you perceive and what you're told, is the entry point for systemic gaslighting. If repeated enough, people start to doubt their own eyes and ears. It becomes so normal that the shock dissipates and acceptance sets in.

Media can amplify all of this. Certain outlets or platforms may subtly (*or overtly*) suggest that only they are trustworthy. Others may present conflicting realities side by side, without context, leaving you flooded and unsure what to believe. Algorithms feed you more of what keeps you engaged – often outrage, fear, or confirmation of your existing bias. They know that fear and divison get more shares, clicks, and ultimately followers.

When you're saturated with contradictory information, it's easy to disconnect from your own knowing. You might either shut down and disengage completely, or cling more tightly to one narrative just to feel stable.

**Examples from Public Figures and Institutions**

We've all watched public figures deny, deflect, or distort reality in real time. While this book isn't about dissecting specific scandals, it's useful to notice the patterns, because they mirror what happens interpersonally, just on a bigger stage.

Common public gaslighting moves include:

- Flatly denying statements or actions that are recorded or documented.
- Reframing harm as "misunderstanding," "over reaction," or "political attacks."
- Blaming whistleblowers or survivors for speaking up.
- Using patriotic, religious, or moral language to position themselves as the victim.
- Shifting the focus from structural issues to individual "bad apples," while leaving systems untouched.

Institutions – whether governmental, educational, corporate, or religious – may gaslight by:

- Claiming "there's no problem here" while quietly settling lawsuits or complaints.
- Making public statements of support while privately retaliating against those who speak out.
- Creating policies that look good on paper but are impossible to assess in practice.
- Releasing carefully crafted narratives that omit key facts or voices.

If you've ever watched a press conference, read a statement, or sat through a company meeting and felt that weird split between the words and the energy, you know this feeling. Your body registers, "Something is off," even if everyone around you is nodding along.

Why does this matter for your personal healing? Because living in a world where public gaslighting is normalized can make you more likely to doubt your own perceptions in private. If you're constantly told, directly or indirectly, that harm isn't harm, that abuse is "just how it is," or that asking for accountability is extremism, it gets harder to trust your internal compass.

**When Reality Feels Like a Moving Target**

One of the most disorienting effects of systemic and public gaslighting is the sensation that reality itself keeps shifting.

In an interpersonal gaslighting dynamic, you might question your memory of a single event. In a larger-scale context, you might start questioning your sense of the world. You hear different "truths" from different sources. Rules seem to change depending on who's in power. What was condemned last year is celebrated this year, or vice versa.

If you're already recovering from relational gaslighting, this can feel like too much. Your nervous system, already sensitized, may respond with anxiety, numbness, or a desire to check out completely.

When reality feels like a moving target, a few things tend to happen:

- You may become hypervigilant, constantly scanning for the "right" position to take so you don't get attacked or excluded.
- You may swing between extremes, fully buying into a narrative and then fully rejecting it, because moderation feels too uncertain.
- You may start to believe that there is no such thing as truth, only power.
- You may feel hopeless, cynical, or deeply alone in what you see.

Energetically, it can feel like being unmoored, floating, dizzy, or disconnected from your own footing. You might find yourself thinking, "I don't know what's real anymore," not just about a relationship, but about the world.

The invitation here is not to find the one "correct" external reality to align with, but to begin building an inner sense of reality that you can trust, even as external narratives shift.

That doesn't mean ignoring facts, isolating from community, or pretending everything is fine. It means practicing:

- Noticing how your body responds to information (*tight, contracted, relaxed, numb*).
- Asking, "Does this feel congruent?" rather than "Do I like this?"
- Being willing to hold complexity: "This part feels true, this part doesn't, and I need to learn more."
- Allowing your views to evolve without shaming yourself for what you used to believe. It's okay to change your mind.

You are not required to have a hot take on everything. You are not required to resolve every contradiction you see. What you are invited to do is honor your awareness, to notice what lands as true for you, what doesn't, and where you may need more information, time, or space.

That is the antidote to gaslighting in the wild. Not certainty for its own sake, but an ongoing, grounded relationship with your own perception.

**End-of-Chapter Exercise: Reclaiming Your Inner Compass**

Take some time with your journal and explore the following prompts:

1. **Pause.** Think of a time when a workplace, community,

or institution dismissed or minimized something you knew was real. Take a moment to bring the situation to mind and write down what happened. As you recall the moment, notice what you felt in your body at the time. Did you feel tension, hesitation, or a sense that something wasn't quite right? Write about what you experienced internally and what story you may have begun telling yourself because of how others responded.

2. **Observe.** Now reflect on the messages you've received from larger systems, such as school, religion, politics, media, or culture, about what is considered "right," "normal," or "acceptable." Write down as many of these messages as you can remember. As you look at your list, circle the ones that have caused you to question or doubt your own experience or perception.

3. **Witness the Pattern.** Think of a public narrative, controversy, or widely discussed issue that left you feeling confused or pulled in different directions. Write out what each "side" of the conversation was saying. Then ask yourself, "What did I actually perceive in that situation? What felt congruent to me, even if I didn't express it out loud?" Notice what becomes clearer when you return to your own awareness.

4. **Exit the Reaction.** Consider how the constant stream of opinions, information, and reactions around you may influence your clarity. Write about one way you could reduce that noise and create more space for your own perception. This might include limiting news or social media for a period of time, choosing a few trusted sources instead of endless scrolling, or taking time to journal before responding to what you see or hear.

5. **Return to Yourself.** Place a hand somewhere on your body – your heart, chest, or belly – and take a slow breath. In your journal or out loud, say: "Even when the world is loud, my awareness matters. I am allowed to trust what I perceive." As you sit with those words, notice any sensations, resistance, or relief that arise, and allow them to be present without judgment.

You can't control how workplaces, religions, politics, or media operate, but you can choose how much of your reality you hand over to them. Every time you turn your attention back to your own knowing, you reclaim a little more of your inner compass and that is something no institution can own.

# PART III: SHUTTING OFF THE GAS

# Chapter 7: Awareness Is the Antidote

By now, you've started to see how gaslighting operates: the tactics, the cycles, the way it gets inside your head and into your body. You've seen how relationships, systems, and even your own inner voice can distort your sense of what's real. That can feel heavy. It can also stir up a lot of reaction.

Anger. Grief. Numbness. The urge to fight. The urge to flee. The urge to fix everything right now.

All of that is valid. And none of it, on its own, is what sets you free.

The real antidote to gaslighting is not more effort, more analysis, or a perfectly crafted comeback. The real antidote to gaslighting is awareness – grounded, present, embodied awareness. Awareness that doesn't need to prove, perform, or convince. Awareness that simply sees what is, without collapsing into it or fighting against it.

This chapter is about that kind of awareness. The kind that lets you notice the hook before it lands. The kind that lets you feel the energy of a situation without getting swallowed by it. The kind that allows you to walk away, not as an act of defeat, but as an act of deep self-respect.

### What Presence Does, That Reaction Can't

When you've been gaslit, your nervous system is often primed for reaction. You've spent so much time defending, explaining, justifying, or trying to make sense of things that the slightest hint of dismissal or distortion can light you up inside. Your body says, "Here we go again," and you're off to the races.

*Reaction isn't wrong.* It's your system trying to protect you, but reaction alone keeps you on the gaslighter's playing field. The moment you spin, they have something to work with: your words, your tone, your tears, your anger. Your reaction becomes the new evidence that you're "too much," "too sensitive," or "the problem."

Presence is different.

Presence is not about being calm and pleasant all the time. Presence is about being *with* what's happening, inside you and around you, without abandoning yourself. It's the moment you feel the familiar surge of panic or shame and, instead of spiraling, you notice it. *You breathe. You stay.*

Where reaction gets swept into the story, presence steps back enough to see the story clearly.

For example, someone says, "You're overreacting, that's not what happened," and your body tightens. The old pattern might be to immediately defend: "Yes it is, you said..." and launch into proving mode. In presence, you still feel that surge, but you recognize it as a cue, not a command. You might think, "*There it is, that familiar drop in my stomach when my reality is dismissed.*" You might take a breath. You might choose not to argue. You might say, "I remember it differently," and leave it there.

***Presence gives you the space to choose.***

Reaction says: "I have to fix this right now so I can feel safe." The only choice is to fix the situation by negating yourself, conforming to the gaslighter's commands and avoiding conflict. Giving in, to get out.

Presence says: "Something feels off. I can trust that and decide what works for me, whether they agree or not." The choice becomes about *you, not them.*

Energetically, presence feels like your awareness filling your own body again. You're not reaching out, chasing, grabbing for validation. You're not leaving yourself to go manage their perception of you. You're here. With you.

From that place, you can notice: "Is this a conversation that is going to go anywhere? Do I actually want to stay and engage? What's the kindest choice for me right now?"

**Awareness Without the Need to Fight or Fix**

When people first start seeing gaslighting clearly, it's common to swing to the opposite extreme.

You might think:

- "Now that I see it, I have to confront every single instance."
- "I need them to admit what they did so I can finally heal."
- "If I don't call this out, I'm abandoning myself."
- "If I just play along, I'm not being authentic to myself."

This is another way gaslighting can hijack your energy even as you're waking up. You can end up in constant battle mode scanning for every slight. Proof-hunting and exhausting yourself trying to make other people own what they may never be willing to see.

***Awareness doesn't require a fight.***

You can be completely aware that someone is gaslighting you and still choose not to engage in a showdown. You can know that a system is unjust and still choose to focus your daily energy on what nourishes you. That's not denial. That's discernment.

There's a difference between suppressing your awareness and choosing how to use it.

Suppressing says: "It's not that bad. I'm overreacting. I should be more forgiving."

Choosing says: "I see what this is. I don't need to make it okay, and I also don't need to exhaust myself trying to change it."

Awareness without the need to fix is:

- Acknowledging to yourself, "That comment was shaming," even if everyone else laughs it off.
- Recognizing, "This policy is unfair," without needing to debate it with every person who benefits from it.
- Noticing, "My body tightens around this person," and honoring that as information, whether or not you can explain it logically.

You're not pretending everything is fine. You're letting

your awareness be real without turning it into your entire job description.

This is especially important if you grew up having to be the fixer, the peacekeeper, or the truth-teller in your family. You may have learned that your worth came from holding everything together or naming what no one else would name. Awareness then became a burden: *if you saw it, you had to deal with it.*

In this book, I'm inviting you into a different relationship with your awareness. One where you can perceive what's happening, honor your knowing, and still choose ease when ease is available.

**Spotting the Hooks Before They Land**

Gaslighters and gaslighting systems rely on hooks.

A hook is the part of the interaction that snags you. It might be a tone, a phrase, a facial expression, or an implication that pokes your most tender places:

- "You're too sensitive."
- "I was just joking."
- "You always do this."
- "Everyone else is fine with it."
- A sigh, an eye roll, a sudden shift into cold

silence.

You feel the hook land in your body as a jolt, a drop, a rush of heat, or a collapse. Before you know it, you're arguing, apologizing, over-explaining, or trying to win back harmony.

Awareness lets you spot the hook *before* you bite.

Instead of only noticing what happened after the argument or after the shame spiral, you start to notice the moment the energy changes. Maybe your chest tightens when they say, "Calm down." Maybe your stomach drops when they say, "I guess I'm just the bad guy again." Maybe your jaw clenches when they bring up how much they've "done for you."

Those body cues are gold. They're your early warning system.

When you feel that shift, you can pause and ask:

- "What just got poked here?"
- "What story are they inviting me to agree to?"
- "Are they trying to get a reaction out of me?"
- "Do I actually have to respond to this?"

Sometimes the most powerful move is not to pick up the

rope.

You might respond with a simple, "I'm not available for this conversation right now." You might change the subject. You might leave the room. You might say nothing at all; not from shutdown, but from choice.

Spotting the hook doesn't mean you'll never get caught again. You're human. There will be times you get pulled in and only realize it later. That's okay. Every time you notice a hook you missed before, your awareness grows. Every time you choose not to bite, the gaslighter's grip loosens just a little more.

### End-of-Chapter Exercise: Practicing Presence in Real Time

Take some time to explore these prompts. You may want to write your responses, or simply sit with them and notice what comes up in your body.

1. **Pause.** Think of a recent situation where you noticed yourself reacting strongly. Perhaps defending yourself, explaining your intentions, or shutting down completely. Take a moment to recall the very first instant when something felt off. In your journal, write about how you recognized it. Was it a specific word, a look, a tone of voice, or a sensation in your body that

alerted you something had shifted?

2. **Observe.** Now reflect on the kinds of moments that tend to pull you into those reactions. Write down three common "hooks" that regularly draw you into old patterns. These might be phrases such as "You're too sensitive," or behaviors like silence, criticism, or dismissal. For each one, describe what happens in your body when it occurs. Do you tense up, feel a rush of energy, or notice your thoughts begin racing?

3. **Witness the Pattern.** As you look at these hooks, consider how often they appear across different relationships or situations. Write about what tends to happen next when one of these moments occurs. What reactions do you usually move into, and what do those reactions lead to in the interaction?

4. **Exit the Reaction.** Now imagine encountering one of those same hooks again, but this time with presence. If you gave yourself even five seconds to breathe before responding, what might change? Write about what you might do differently and what choices could become available if you allowed the moment to pause rather than reacting immediately.

5. **Return to Yourself.** Place a hand somewhere on

your body – your heart, chest, or belly – and take a slow breath. In your journal or out loud, say: "My awareness is enough. I don't have to prove what I know to anyone in order for it to be real." Notice any sensations, resistance, or relief that arise, and allow them to be present without trying to change them.

***Awareness is not something you earn. It's something you already have.***

The more you practice being present with yourself in the tension, in the confusion, in the clarity, the less room gaslighting has to operate. You don't have to fight your way out. You can simply *stop leaving you.*

# Chapter 8: Shifting from Victim to Source

If gaslighting is designed to make you doubt your reality, then one of the most radical things you can do is reclaim yourself as the source of it.

That doesn't mean you created the abuse. It doesn't mean you "manifested" the harm or chose the distortion. What it does mean is this: *you* are the only one who can choose how you relate to what has happened, what you make it mean, and what you create from here.

Gaslighting trains you into a position of energetic victimhood, not just in the sense of being harmed, but in the sense of being at the mercy of other people's stories. Your sense of self becomes reactive instead of generative. You're constantly responding to what they say, what they do, what they withhold, and what they deny, rather than chasing what you truly desire.

Shifting from victim to source is not about blaming

yourself. It's about recognizing that your awareness, your perception, and your choices are not small, fragile things. They are the engine of your life. When you begin to live from that awareness, gaslighting loses its grip. Not because other people suddenly become kind and honest, but because you stop outsourcing your reality to them.

In this chapter, we'll explore the energetic mechanics of taking your power back, the questions that reconnect you with what you know, and the process of rebuilding trust in your own perception and choices.

### The Energetic Mechanics of Taking Your Power Back

Energetically, gaslighting works by pulling your attention outward and away from you.

Instead of asking, "What do I notice? What feels true for me?" your focus gets hooked into questions like:

- "Do they believe me?"
- "Did I say it the right way?"
- "How do I prove I'm not what they say I am?"

Your energy leaves your body and orients around them – their moods, their interpretations, their approval. Over time, this can feel like living slightly outside of yourself, always scanning for signals about whether you or the situation is okay. Maybe you're walking on eggshells or questioning what version of your partner is going to get out of bed that day. Whatever the experience is, every choice is oriented around not upsetting them.

***Taking your power back is, at its core, an energetic reorientation.***

It's the moment you notice, "My attention is over there again, trying to manage their perception," and you gently bring it home. You move from asking, "How do I get them to see me?" to "What do I see?" From "How do I get them to choose me?" to "What am I choosing for me?"

This shift is subtle but profound. You may still feel the pull to explain or defend... that's normal. But instead of obeying that pull automatically, you begin to recognize it as a well-worn groove, not a requirement.

Think of it like this: when you're in victim mode (*through no fault of your own*), your energy runs outward on a loop. It goes toward the gaslighter, the system, the story, and never quite makes it back to you. When you're the source, your energy circulates through you. You can still perceive others, care about them, and respond to them, but you don't leave yourself to do it.

Being the source doesn't mean you control everything. It means you recognize that your awareness and your choices are the starting point of your reality, not an afterthought. For many people, that shift doesn't happen all at once. It begins in small, almost ordinary moments, when you stop overriding yourself and start listening to what is actually true for you.

### Client Case Scenario: Small Choices to Take Power Back

For Michael, it started quietly. For a long time, he believed the biggest problem in his life was that he couldn't trust himself. He second-guessed everything: what he felt, what he remembered, what he wanted, even what kind of coffee he ordered. He had spent years in relationships and environments where other people's certainty always overrode his awareness. If someone questioned him, he folded. If someone was disappointed, he assumed he was wrong. He described himself as "bad at life," but what he really meant was, "I don't know how to hear myself anymore."

At first, his healing didn't look dramatic. It looked small. He started noticing when his body tightened before saying yes to something he didn't actually want to do. He practiced pausing before answering. He let himself choose the restaurant he actually wanted, instead of saying, "I'm fine with anything." He stopped asking three friends what they thought before making every little decision. Then those small choices started becoming bigger ones. He left conversations that felt demeaning instead of staying to prove his point. He stopped over-explaining himself at work. He noticed which people left him feeling more like himself and which ones left him confused and diminished.

Over time, Michael's whole life began to revolve around one quiet shift: he stopped treating his awareness like an inconvenience and started treating it like information. And the more he honored those small, self-honoring choices, the less broken he felt – and the more he began to realize he had never actually lost himself. He had simply been trained to abandon himself.

### Asking: What Do I Know Here? What's My Reality?

One of the simplest and most powerful ways to shift from victim to source is to start asking different questions.

Gaslighting trains you to ask, "What do they think? What do they remember? What do they say is true? What are they going to do?" You learn to defer to external authority, even when that authority is clearly not acting in your best interest.

To reclaim your reality, you begin asking instead:

- "What do I know here?"
- "What do I perceive?"
- "How is this affecting my body?"
- "If I weren't trying to make them right, what would be obvious?"

These questions are not about building a legal case. They're about reconnecting you with your own awareness.

For example, someone might tell you, "You're making a big deal out of nothing." Instead of automatically scanning for how to tone yourself down, you pause and check: "Does this feel like nothing to me? What impact does it actually have?" You might notice a tightness in your chest, a heaviness in your belly, or a wave of sadness. *That's real data.*

Or a workplace might insist, "We value everyone equally here," while consistently overlooking your contributions. You can acknowledge: "The words say one thing. The pattern says another. My reality includes both."

Asking, "What's my reality?" doesn't require you to convince anyone else to agree with it. It's about giving yourself permission to let your perception count.

You might write out your version of events, not as a document to send them, but as a way of saying to yourself, "I was there. I saw what I saw. I felt what I felt." You might note the ways you minimized or explained things away at the time, and what you notice now with more distance.

The more you practice this, the less interested you become in debates about whether your reality is acceptable to others. You start to anchor into a quieter, steadier sense of knowing: "I may not have all the details perfectly remembered, but I trust my overall perception of how this impacted me."

**Reclaiming Trust in Your Perception and Choice**

Gaslighting doesn't just shake your trust in other people. It shakes your *trust in yourself.*

You might find yourself thinking:

- "I can't tell what's real anymore."
- "I always pick the wrong people."
- "I shouldn't be allowed to make big decisions."

These conclusions are understandable. When your perception has been consistently dismissed or distorted, it makes sense that you'd start doubting it. But here's the truth: your capacity to perceive didn't disappear. It got buried under layers of training to override it.

***Reclaiming trust in your perception starts small.***

You don't have to begin with life-altering choices. You can begin with everyday, low-stakes moments:

- "Do I actually want to go to this event, or do I feel like I should?"
- "Does my body feel more relaxed around this person, or more tense?"
- "If I weren't afraid of disappointing anyone, what would I choose right now?"

Each time you notice what you perceive and how you act in alignment with it, even in tiny ways, you send yourself a message: "I hear you. You matter."

Trust in your choices rebuilds the same way.

You may be afraid of choosing "wrong" again. You may worry that healing means you'll somehow become immune to ever being misled or hurt, and since you can't guarantee that, you feel stuck.

Instead of pressuring yourself to choose perfectly, what if you aimed to choose kindly? To ask, "Is this choice kind to me?" rather than, "Is this choice guaranteed to work out?" Kindness might mean giving yourself more time. It might mean setting a small boundary instead of a massive one. It might mean leaving a conversation when your body is screaming "enough," even if your mind doesn't have all the logic yet.

As you do this, your identity begins to shift. You're no longer just the person things happen to. You're the person who responds, who chooses, who creates.

You still acknowledge the harm. You still honor what was done to you. And you also start to feel the quiet, powerful truth that you are more than what was done. You are a being with awareness, with perception, with the ability to choose again and again.

That is what it means to move from victim to source. Not to erase your story, but to stop letting it be the only thing that defines what's possible for you.

**End-of-Chapter Exercise: From Victim to Source**

Set aside some quiet time with your journal and explore the following prompts. Go gently. This isn't about forcing yourself into empowerment. It's about getting curious about where your power already lives.

1. **Pause.** Think of an area of your life where you still feel like a victim of someone else's story. Take a moment to slow down and write about the situation as honestly as you can. What happened? How did it impact you? As you reflect, notice what story you may have begun telling yourself about who you were in that experience.

2. **Observe.** Now gently ask yourself, "What do I know here that I've been trained to ignore?" As you sit with the question, notice any sensations in your body, images, memories, or phrases that come to mind. You don't need to analyze or explain them. Simply write down whatever arises.

3. **Witness the Pattern.** Consider how this experience may have influenced the way you see yourself or your choices in other parts of your life. Write about any patterns you notice – moments where the same story, doubt, or hesitation appears again in relationships, decisions, or opportunities.

4. **Exit the Reaction.** Identify one small area where you can begin bringing your attention back to yourself. This might be something simple, like checking in with your body before agreeing to plans, noticing how

you feel after spending time with certain people, or pausing before responding out of obligation. Write about one way you could begin shifting your attention back to your own awareness.

5. **Return to Yourself.** Place a hand somewhere on your body – your heart, chest, or belly – and take a slow breath. In your journal or out loud, say: "I am allowed to be the source of my own reality. I don't have to prove my knowing to anyone in order for it to count." Notice what happens in your system as you say these words. Tightness, resistance, ease, or relief may all arise, and whatever appears is welcome here.

Shifting from victim to source is not a one-time event. It's a series of small, everyday choices to bring your energy, your attention, and your trust back to you. Each time you do, you turn down the volume on gaslighting and turn up the volume on your own life.

# Chapter 9: Boundaries without Defense

If gaslighting is about hijacking your reality, boundaries are about reclaiming it.

For many people coming out of gaslighting, the word "boundaries" can feel loaded. Maybe you were told your boundaries were selfish, dramatic, or mean. Maybe every time you tried to set one, it turned into a fight, or the silent treatment. Maybe you learned that the only way to be safe was to either have no boundaries at all, or to build walls so high that no one could get close.

Boundaries without defense are something different.

They are not about explaining yourself into exhaustion. They are not about convincing the gaslighter to agree that your limits are reasonable. They're not about winning. Boundaries without defense are a quiet, grounded knowing of what you will and will not participate in, and a willingness to act on that, whether or not the other person understands, agrees, or approves.

In this chapter, we'll look at what it means to make a gaslighter truly irrelevant. How to use their own obsession with image to disrupt control and what it looks like to say, "I see you" without collapsing, reacting, or losing yourself.

### Making Them Irrelevant without Needing to "Win"

One of the most painful legacies of gaslighting is the feeling that you are always on trial.

Every interaction can feel like a case you have to win: you gather evidence, you rehearse conversations in your head, you anticipate their counterarguments. If they twist your words, you work harder to say it "right." If they deny what happened, you dig for more proof. Your nervous system stays geared for battle, even when you're exhausted.

This is not a failure on your part, it's a survival strategy. When someone keeps rewriting reality, of course you try to defend it. Of course you want to win the argument, or at least be heard for the truth as you know it. If you can just get them to see it, then maybe you won't have to live in that fog anymore.

That "fog" many people describe after gaslighting has a

name: cognitive fog. Cognitive fog is the mental cloudiness that develops when someone has been exposed to chronic confusion, contradiction, and emotional stress over time.

When your reality is repeatedly questioned or rewritten, your brain has to work overtime to track what happened, compare versions of events, anticipate reactions, and protect against further conflict. That kind of ongoing strain can affect concentration, memory, decision-making, and mental clarity. You may lose your train of thought, replay conversations compulsively, struggle to organize what you know, or feel unable to trust your own conclusions even when something is clearly off.

In gaslighting dynamics, cognitive fog is not just a feeling. It is often part of how the control works. The more mentally overloaded you become, the harder it is to stay rooted in your own awareness. Instead of thinking clearly from your own center, you get pulled into constant sorting, proving, self-correcting, and trying to make incoherent behavior make sense. Over time, the nervous system and mind both start to tire.

That exhaustion can make the gaslighter seem more believable, not because they are telling the truth, but because your system is depleted. The fog is not proof that you're broken. It is often the predictable result of trying to stay oriented inside a reality that keeps being distorted. And when you've spent enough time in that kind of confusion, it makes perfect sense that part of you starts believing clarity will only come if you can finally get them to admit the truth.

But here's the hard and freeing truth: *you don't have to win to get free.*

You don't need the gaslighter to admit what happened. You don't need them to validate your experience. You don't even need them to understand you. What you need is your own clarity and the willingness to make choices from it.

Making someone irrelevant doesn't mean pretending they don't exist. It means their opinion no longer determines your reality, your worth, or your next move.

Practically, this might look like shifting from arguments to actions:

- Instead of debating whether their comment was hurtful, you notice how you feel and decide whether you want to end the conversation.
- Instead of trying to prove you're not "too

sensitive," you honor that your system is reacting and give yourself space.

- Instead of explaining why a boundary is valid, you simply state it once and follow through.

For example, rather than saying, "You're gaslighting me and I need you to stop," you might say, "I'm not available for this kind of conversation," and then hang up, leave the room, or change the subject. You might let their texts go unanswered. You might stop giving detailed explanations and simply say, "That doesn't work for me."

Notice that none of these examples require the other person to agree with you.

Boundaries without defense are less about getting them to do something different, and more about you choosing something different – where you put your time, your attention, your body, your energy.

Energetically, this feels like pulling your power back from their courtroom. You stop showing up as the defendant. You stop taking the stand. You stop asking for a verdict. You recognize that the trial was never going to be fair in the first place, and you walk out of the room.

**Client Case Scenario: No Need to Defend**

For Jordan, this shift didn't begin with one dramatic boundary. It began with availability. For years, every call with a parent felt like a trial. If Jordan shared something vulnerable, it was minimized. If hurt was named, it was denied or turned back around. If Jordan tried to clarify what had actually happened, the conversation spiraled into blame, confusion, and the familiar pressure to defend themself.

Jordan used to stay on the phone long after their body had started tightening, trying to find the right words, the right tone, the right proof that would finally make the other person understand. It never worked. They would hang up and leave shaky, exhausted, and full of cognitive fog, already rehearsing what they should have said differently.

What changed was not the content of the conversations, but Jordan's willingness to stop participating in them the same way. They started making the calls shorter. They stopped answering every text right away. When the tone shifted into criticism or rewriting reality, Jordan said, "I'm going to get off the phone now," and did. They didn't announce a whole new philosophy. They didn't try to make the other person agree with their boundaries. They simply became less available for distortion.

At first, it felt cruel. Then it felt unfamiliar. Eventually, it felt like relief. The external dynamic didn't transform overnight, but something inside Jordan did. They stopped feeling like they had to win every case brought against them. They began to trust that leaving the courtroom was not avoidance. It was self-respect.

### Using the Gaslighter's Obsession with Image to Disrupt Control

Many gaslighters care deeply about how they appear to others.

They may present as charming, generous, spiritual, helpful, or morally superior in public, while behaving very differently in private. Their image is part of how they maintain control: if everyone else sees them as "wonderful," it becomes harder for you to trust your experience of their harm.

You are not responsible for managing their image. That's not your job. But you can stop colluding with it.

Colluding with their image might look like laughing off their behavior in front of others, covering for them when they cross a line, or downplaying what's happening because you don't want to seem "dramatic." It might look like staying silent when someone else describes them in a way that doesn't match your reality, because speaking up feels too risky.

Again, there is no shame in any of this. You did what you needed to do to survive. And, as your awareness grows, you may find there are ways to let their own behavior speak for itself.

Using their obsession with image to disrupt control doesn't mean launching a smear campaign or trying to destroy their reputation. It means shifting where and how you're willing to engage.

For example, you might:

- Choose to only have certain conversations in writing (*emails, messages*) so there is a record, rather than letting them rewrite everything later.
- Suggest bringing a neutral third party into key discussions (*a therapist, mediator, HR representative, or trusted friend*) knowing they are less likely to say the most extreme things in front of an audience.
- Calmly say, "I'd like to talk about this when we're with the counselor," rather than hashing it out alone where they feel most free to distort.

You're not doing this to trap them. You're creating

conditions where you don't have to hold the entire truth by yourself. In some cases, simply refusing to participate in their private version of reality is enough to shift the dynamic

If they lie about you to others, you don't have to go on a tour correcting every person. You might choose a few key people to be honest with, and then let time and patterns reveal the rest. Remember: a gaslighter's image is their project, not yours.

Your project is your reality, your healing, your nervous system, your life. Every time you decline to polish their mask for them, you're bringing your energy back to where it belongs.

### Saying "I See You" without Reaction or Collapse

One of the most powerful inner shifts you can make is moving from "What if I'm wrong about them?" to "I see you."

You may never say those words out loud. This isn't about dramatic showdowns or monologues, it's about an internal stance. A quiet, steady recognition of the pattern in front of you.

"I see you" might sound like this, inside your own mind:

- "I see that you're twisting my words to avoid responsibility."
- "I see that you're using silence to punish and control."
- "I see that you're charming in public and cruel in private."
- "I see that you're more invested in being right than in being real."

You're naming what is, for you, without needing them to agree.

The key is doing this without collapsing into helplessness and without escalating into reactive attack.

Collapse sounds like: "I see you, and I guess this is just how it will always be. There's nothing I can do."

Attack sounds like: "I see you, and I'm going to expose, fix, or punish you until you change."

Both keep you energetically tied to them.

"I see you" without reaction or collapse sounds more like: "I see what this is. I'm not making it my job to change it. And I'm not making it my fault. I'm simply letting this information guide my choices."

From this place, your boundaries become clearer:

- You may choose to limit contact or end it entirely.
- You may stop sharing vulnerable information with someone who consistently weaponizes it.
- You may stop explaining your every move and start letting your actions speak.

You don't need a big exit speech. You don't need a perfectly worded explanation. You don't need them to acknowledge that you see them. Your nervous system registers the shift: "I am no longer pretending not to know what I know."

Energetically, saying "I see you" is like turning the light on in a room you've been stumbling through in the dark. The furniture hasn't changed. The walls are the same. But now you can navigate without constantly crashing into things and wondering if you're the problem. *You're not.*

You are someone who sees clearly. And you are someone who gets to choose what to do with that clarity.

### End-of-Chapter Exercise: Boundaries without Defense

Use these prompts to explore what boundaries without defense might look like for you. Go at your own pace. You don't have to implement anything immediately; simply noticing is a powerful start.

1. **Pause.** Think of an area of your life where you still find yourself trying to "win" with a gaslighter or within a gaslighting system. Take a moment to slow down and recall a recent interaction. In your journal, describe what happened and notice how much of your energy went into proving your point, explaining yourself, or trying to get the other person to agree with you.

2. **Observe.** Now imagine stepping out of their courtroom entirely. If you were no longer trying to win the argument or gain their validation, what boundary might become clear? Write about what boundary you might set or strengthen – this could involve how much contact you have, which topics you are willing to discuss, or how long you remain in certain environments.

3. **Witness the Pattern.** Reflect on whether there are ways you may have been colluding with someone's image against your own reality. This could look like minimizing their behavior, covering for them, or staying silent to keep the peace. Write about where

you notice this pattern and how it may have affected your trust in your own perception.

4. **Exit the Reaction.** Write the phrase "I see you" at the top of a page in your journal. Underneath it, list the patterns you now recognize in a particular person or system. Allow yourself to be honest on the page. You don't have to show this to anyone. This exercise is simply a way of acknowledging what you see without needing to argue or defend it.

5. **Return to Yourself.** Place a hand somewhere on your body – your heart, chest, or belly – and take a slow breath. In your journal or out loud, say: "My boundaries don't need your approval to be valid. I am allowed to choose what I participate in." Notice what happens inside you as you say these words. Tightness, resistance, or relief may arise, and whatever you experience is welcome.

Boundaries without defense are not about becoming hard or untouchable. They're about becoming so rooted in your own reality that you no longer need to fight for it in every room.

***You know what you know. You choose what you choose. And that is enough.***

# PART IV: BUILDING A LIFE BEYOND GASLIGHTING

# Chapter 10: Shutting Off the Gas, Every Day

Shutting off the gas isn't a single moment of clarity where everything magically resets and you never doubt yourself again.

It's daily.

It's the small, steady choices you make to come back to you, again and again, no matter how loud other people's stories get. It's how you start your morning, how you speak to yourself when you're triggered, how you respond when someone questions your reality, and how you wind down at night.

This chapter is about integrating everything you've been reading into the rhythm of your life. Not as a rigid checklist, but as a living practice.

We'll explore practical tools and awareness check-ins you can use to stay connected to your reality. We'll look at what it means to create a life that isn't up for debate. And how your happiness, your thriving, and your ease can become a powerful form of resistance to gaslighting of any kind.

### Practical Tools and Awareness Check-Ins

When you've lived in gaslighting dynamics, everyday life can become a minefield of second-guessing. A message left unread. A comment that lands funny. An unexpected change of plans. Your body remembers what it was like when small things turned into big explosions, or subtle but relentless distortions.

Daily practices give your nervous system a new rhythm to lean into. They're not about controlling everything that happens around you. They're about giving yourself anchors you can return to when the old patterns try to pull you back in.

Here are some simple tools you can weave into your day:

1. **Morning check-in.** Before you reach for your phone, take a few breaths and ask:
    - "What am I aware of today?"
    - "What do I need today?"
    - "What would be kind to me today?"

You don't have to come up with profound answers. Just

notice whatever arises. Sensations, words, a sense of heaviness or lightness. You're starting the day by listening to you, rather than immediately tuning into everyone else's reality.

2. **Body scan breaks.** Set a reminder a few times a day to pause and check in with your body:

    - "Where am I tense?"
    - "Where am I relaxed?"
    - "What am I carrying that isn't mine?"

If you notice tightness that feels like someone else's energy or expectations, imagine gently handing it back, not as blame, but as release. You don't have to hold what isn't yours.

3. **Reality check questions.** When you feel yourself spiraling into doubt after an interaction, ask:

    - "What actually happened?" (*Just the observable facts.*)
    - "What did I feel in my body?"
    - "What story am I telling myself about this?"

Writing this down can help separate the event from the layers of meaning you might be piling on out of habit.

4. **Somatic reset.** When you feel heavy, foggy, or activated, press your feet firmly into the floor and gently press your hands into your thighs or together. Then shake out your hands, arms, or shoulders for a few seconds and slowly look around the room, naming 3 – 5 things you can see. Let your body register: "I'm here. I can come back to myself now."

5. **End-of-day debrief.** Before bed, ask yourself:

    - "Where did I stay connected to me today?"
    - "Where did I leave myself?"
    - "What am I proud of?"

This isn't a performance review. It's a gentle way to notice your progress, acknowledge your courage, and see where you might choose differently tomorrow.

### Creating a Reality That Isn't up for Debate

"Creating a reality that isn't up for debate" doesn't mean you stop listening to feedback or that you never change your mind. It means you no longer outsource the core of your reality – your perception, your needs, your values – to other people's approval.

In gaslighting dynamics, almost everything about you can become negotiable: what you saw, what you felt, whether your boundaries are "reasonable," whether your memories are accurate. Over time, you can start treating your entire inner world like a courtroom exhibit that has to be defended.

Your daily practices are how you walk out of that courtroom and start decorating your own house instead.

Practically, creating a reality that isn't up for debate might look like:

- Keeping a private record of significant events, conversations, or decisions. Not to build a case against anyone, but to honor your own memory and perception.
- Naming your feelings to yourself without immediately arguing with them. "I feel hurt. I feel dismissed. I feel unseen." You can later decide what, if anything, you want to do with that awareness.
- Clarifying your non-negotiables in relationships: "I don't stay in conversations where my reality is mocked or denied. I don't explain my boundaries more than once." These are for you first. You may or may not share them out loud.
- Choosing a few trusted people, friends,

professionals, community members, who have shown they can hold your reality with care, and leaning into those spaces when you start to doubt yourself.

You're gradually shifting from "Is my reality acceptable?" to "This is my reality. What would I like to choose from here?"

Energetically, creating a reality that isn't up for debate feels like a deepening inside your own life. You're less interested in arguing about your experience and more interested in living it. You spend less time rehearsing imaginary conversations and more time doing things that actually nourish you – walking, reading, creating, resting, connecting with people who feel good.

Gaslighting thrives in the gap between *what you know* and what you're *willing to stand by*. Every time you close that gap, even a little, you turn down the gas.

### When Happiness Becomes Your Best Form of Resistance

Gaslighting wants you small, confused, and dependent. It wants you doubting your joy, questioning your desires, and apologizing for your needs. It wants you so preoccupied with proving your reality that you forget you came here to live a life, not just survive someone else's.

***One of the most potent ways to shut off the gas is to reclaim your right to be happy.***

Not performative happiness, not forced positivity, but genuine moments of pleasure, ease, and satisfaction that have nothing to do with convincing anyone of anything.

Happiness as resistance looks like:

- Laughing freely without worrying whether someone will call you "too much."
- Enjoying a quiet evening alone without making it mean you're unlovable.
- Allowing yourself hobbies, rest, and beauty even if no one else understands why they matter to you.
- Letting yourself receive kindness without immediately minimizing it or waiting for the other shoe to drop.

For many survivors of gaslighting, happiness can feel dangerous at first. Joy may have been followed by punishment or withdrawal. Success may have been met with envy or sabotage. So part of your "daily shutting off the gas" is gently expanding your capacity to let good things in without bracing for impact.

You don't have to start with "I'm ecstatic about my life." You can start with:

- "Today, I'm going to notice one thing that feels good and let myself enjoy it for ten extra seconds."
- "Today, I'm going to do one small thing just because it delights me."
- "Today, I'm going to let myself feel proud of one choice I made."

The more you allow yourself to experience real moments of happiness, the less appealing it becomes to reenter dynamics that thrive on your suffering. The contrast gets clearer: "When I'm with this person or in this environment, I shrink. When I'm in my own life, choosing what lights me up, I expand."

Your thriving is not a betrayal of your past self or of others who are still in the fog. It's a signal – a living, breathing example that another reality is possible.

You don't have to use your happiness to prove anything to anyone. You can simply live it. And in doing so, you become harder and harder to gaslight, because you have too much evidence of your own truth to trade it for someone else's lie.

**End-of-Chapter Exercise: Daily Ways to Shut Off the Gas**

This exercise is an invitation to translate the ideas in this chapter into daily, doable practices. Let it be simple and kind.

1. **Design your morning anchor.** Write down one question or practice you'd like to start your day with for the next week (*for example, a three-breath check-in, a journaling question, or a body scan*). Imagine how your day would change if you began listening to yourself first instead of others.

2. **Name your non-debatable truths.** List three things about your reality that you are no longer willing to argue about, feelings, needs, values, or experiences. You don't have to share this list with anyone else. This is for you.

3. **Identify your daily clearings.** Notice one recurring situation that tends to leave you feeling foggy or heavy (*a certain conversation, environment, or task*). What simple phrase, breath, or movement could you use afterward to clear some of that energy and come back to yourself?

4. **Map your happiness.** List five small things that

genuinely bring you ease or joy. Things that are available to you now, not someday in a perfect future. Circle one you can choose today. Then actually choose it, and notice what happens in your body when you let yourself have that moment.

5. **Create a daily reminder.** Write a sentence on a sticky note, in your phone, or in your journal: "My reality is not up for debate. My happiness is not a problem to solve." Place it somewhere you'll see it. Each time you read it, take one conscious breath.

Shutting off the gas every day isn't about never getting triggered or never doubting yourself again. It's about building a life where your awareness, your boundaries, and your joy have more say than any gaslighter ever did.

***One choice at a time, you're creating a reality that belongs to you.***

# Chapter 11: Choosing Conscious Relationships

As you begin to reclaim your reality, a natural question arises: "What now?"

You've seen how gaslighting operates. You've started to recognize the patterns in your past and present. You may have left relationships, shifted dynamics, or created boundaries that once felt impossible. And underneath all of that work is often a quieter, more tender desire:

"I don't want to go through this again. I want something different."

This chapter is about that "something different."

Choosing conscious relationships doesn't mean finding perfect people who never hurt you, never misunderstand you, and never have their own blind spots. It means choosing people and dynamics where awareness, honesty, and mutual respect matter more than control, image, or being right. It means being willing to bring you – your needs, your perceptions, your questions – into connection, instead of disappearing to keep the peace.

We'll explore how *NOT* to recreate gaslighting dynamics, what friendship, love, and collaboration can look like beyond control, and the difference between what you deserve and what you accept.

**How Not to Recreate Gaslighting Dynamics**

One of the most uncomfortable truths about healing from gaslighting is realizing how easy it can be to slip back into similar patterns even with different people and in different contexts.

This does not mean you're broken or destined to repeat the same story forever. It means your nervous system has a template it recognizes. Intensity can still feel like love. Over-responsibility can still feel like caring. Walking on eggshells can still feel normal.

The goal isn't to shame yourself for those tendencies. The goal is to notice them sooner and choose differently.

Here are some early signs you may be sliding into a familiar gaslighting-style dynamic:

- You start explaining yourself more and

more, but feel understood less and less.

- You minimize your own discomfort because you don't want to "make a big deal out of it."
- Your body tightens around conversations where you give feedback or express a need.
- You feel responsible for managing the other person's moods, reactions, or image.
- You regularly leave interactions feeling smaller, confused, or doubting yourself.

You might notice these signs in romantic relationships, friendships, work collaborations, or community spaces. The context changes, but the sensation of losing yourself to keep the connection stays eerily similar.

Not recreating gaslighting dynamics doesn't mean never feeling discomfort or conflict. Conscious relationships will still bring up your stuff. The difference is what happens next.

In a repeating gaslighting pattern, discomfort leads to distortion: your feelings are dismissed, blamed, or turned back on you. In conscious relationships, discomfort becomes an opening for curiosity, conversation and repair.

You might say, "When that happened, I felt dismissed,"

and instead of hearing, "You're overreacting," you hear, "I didn't realize that. Tell me more." Or even, "Ouch, I feel defensive, but I want to understand. Can we slow down?"

You don't need people who never trigger you. You need people who are willing to look with you when something feels off without making you wrong for noticing.

| Gaslighting | Conscious Relationship |
|---|---|
| Your reality is questioned. | Your reality is respected. |
| Conflict creates confusion. | Conflict can lead to repair. |
| You feel pressure to prove yourself. | You can express yourself clearly. |
| Boundaries are treated as a threat. | Boundaries are part of care. |
| You leave feeling smaller. | You leave feeling more like yourself. |
| Connection feels conditional. | Connection makes room for you. |

## Friendship, Love, and Collaboration Beyond Control

So what does it look like when relationships are based on presence and choice, rather than control and gaslighting?

It's tempting to answer with a list of behaviors: they listen, they apologize, they take responsibility. Those things matter. But underneath them is an energetic quality that's even more important: *space.*

In conscious relationships, there is space for:

- Two or more realities to be acknowledged, even when they don't match perfectly.
- Feelings to be expressed without being instantly fixed, dismissed, or weaponized.
- Boundaries to be set without the relationship being threatened every time.
- Growth and change, rather than rigid roles that must be maintained.

Friendship beyond control might look like a friend who can say, "Hey, that hurt," and also hear it when you say the same. It might be someone who doesn't keep score of who called or texted last, but does notice if the energy between you feels off and is willing to check in.

Love beyond control might look like, a partner who can tolerate your "no" without turning it into a referendum on your love for them. Someone who can admit when they've been unfair, and who cares about repairing, not to restore their image, but *because your connection matters.*

Collaboration beyond control might look like work or

creative partnerships where disagreement is not a threat, but part of the process. Where questions and feedback are welcomed, not punished. Where you're not expected to abandon your values to belong.

None of this means the people involved are perfectly healed or always grateful. It means there is a shared commitment to curiosity over control, repair over retaliation, and truth over appearances.

One helpful question to ask yourself is: "Do I feel more like myself, or less like myself, when I'm with this person or group?"

In gaslighting dynamics, you learn to contort – to be smaller, quieter, more agreeable, less "difficult." In conscious relationships, you may feel stretched, challenged, or seen in new ways, but you don't have to disappear. The relationship makes more space for you, not less.

**What You Desire vs. What You Accept**

Gaslighting has a way of lowering your bar.

When you're repeatedly told that you're too sensitive, too much, or the problem, you may start to believe that basic respect and emotional safety are luxuries you haven't earned. You might think, consciously or not:

- "This is as good as it gets for me."
- "Everyone is like this, I just need to toughen up."
- "If I leave, I'll be alone. At least this is something."

Over time, what you accept as "normal" can drift far away from what you actually desire.

Let's be clear: you deserve relationships where your reality is not up for constant debate. Where your "no" is heard as a complete sentence, not a starting point for negotiation. Where you are not required to sacrifice your self-trust in order to stay connected.

Deserving this is not something you earn by being good enough, forgiving enough, spiritual enough, or healed enough. You deserve it because you exist. Because you are a person with a nervous system, a heart, a history, and a life.

The harder question is often: "What am I still accepting?"

This is where awareness meets choice. You may find yourself noticing, "I know I desire more than this, and I'm not ready to leave yet." That's okay. Forcing yourself into choices before you're ready can recreate the same sense of pressure you experienced in gaslighting dynamics.

Instead, you might gently track:

- "What am I tolerating that doesn't feel good to me?"
- "What story am I telling myself about why I have to accept this or why I deserve this?"
- "What would shift if I believed, even 5%, that I deserve kindness and clarity here?"

As you raise your internal sense of what is acceptable, you may notice relationships falling away or reshaping themselves. Some people will step up when you stop shrinking. Others won't. Your task is not to control their response. Your task is to stay in integrity with what you now know you desire.

Choosing conscious relationships is not about curating a perfect inner circle. It's about refusing to abandon yourself to keep a place in someone else's story.

**End-of-Chapter Exercise: Creating Space for Conscious Connections**

Take some time to sit with these prompts. Let your responses be imperfect, evolving, and honest.

1. **Pause.** Think of a current or recent relationship – romantic, platonic, family, or work – and take a

moment to slow down and reflect on it honestly. In your journal, write about the ways this relationship feels similar to past gaslighting dynamics and the ways it feels different. As you do, note any early warning signs you've noticed, as well as any moments that show genuine openness, accountability, or repair.

2. **Observe.** Create two columns in your journal titled "What I Accepted" and "What I Desire." In the first column, list behaviors, dynamics, or patterns you have tolerated in the past that did not honor you. In the second column, write what you now recognize you desire instead. As you look at the two lists side by side, notice what emotions or insights arise.

3. **Witness the Pattern.** Now recall a moment – even a small one – when you felt deeply yourself with another person. Write about what was happening in that interaction and how your body felt in their presence. As you reflect, consider what was different about that moment compared with interactions that left you doubting yourself.

4. **Exit the Reaction.** Think about one small boundary or request you could bring into a current relationship to make it more conscious. This might involve asking

for more notice before plans, requesting a pause when conversations become heated, or sharing honestly about how certain comments land for you. Write about what it might feel like to express that boundary, even if you are not ready to act on it immediately.

5. **Return to Yourself.** Place a hand somewhere on your body – your heart, chest, or belly – and take a slow breath. In your journal or out loud, say: "I am worthy of relationships where my reality is welcome. I am allowed to choose people and spaces that make more room for me, not less." Notice what happens in your system as you say these words. Whether you feel resistance, relief, or both, allow whatever arises to be there without judgment.

Conscious relationships don't require you to be perfectly healed. They invite you to bring your awareness, your boundaries, and your truth into connection. As you do, the people and spaces that can meet you there will become clearer... and so will the ones that can't.

# Chapter 12: Recovery Isn't Linear

By the time you reach this point in the book, you may have already noticed something about your own process: *it's not moving in a straight line.*

Some days, you might feel clear, strong, and grounded in your reality. Other days, a text, a memory, a smell, or a social media post can send you right back into doubt, grief, or shame. There might be mornings when you feel proud of the boundaries you've set, and nights when you wonder if you made everything up.

This doesn't mean you're *failing.* It means you're *healing.*

Recovery from gaslighting is not a neat sequence of "understand, leave, heal, move on." It's more like a spiral. You revisit themes. Old feelings resurface at new depths. You catch patterns sooner than you used to, but that doesn't mean they never show up. You may still have days when you miss the person who hurt you, or wish the story had ended differently.

In this chapter, we'll explore the non-linear nature of recovery. The grief and regret that often arise, the myth of wasted time, and how to heal without judgment. We'll also look at what it means to start including yourself in your choices again, even when you don't feel perfectly "over it."

**Grief, Regret, and the Myth of Wasted Time**

Gaslighting doesn't just distort your perception while you're in it. It can also color how you look back on your entire life.

Once you start to see the pattern, it's common to feel a wave of regret:

- "What was I thinking?"
- "Why didn't I leave sooner?"
- "How could I have believed them for so long?"
- "I wasted years of my life."

These thoughts can be brutal. They can make it hard to celebrate your progress because you're so focused on what you wish you'd done differently. Underneath the regret, though, is usually grief.

Grief for the version of you who kept trying. Grief for the opportunities you passed by because you were busy managing someone else's reality. Grief for the love you offered that wasn't met. Grief for the time, energy, and care you gave in good faith.

***Grief is not a sign that you're stuck. It's a sign that you're telling yourself the truth about what happened and what it cost you.***

The idea of "wasted time" can be one more way you gaslight yourself. When you say, "I wasted ten years," you erase the person who lived those years. The one who did their best with the information and tools they had. You make yourself wrong for not having the awareness you only gained by going through what you went through.

What if, instead of deciding those years were wasted, you acknowledged them as part of your training in awareness? Not training you asked for. Not training you would ever wish on anyone. But training that has given you a level of perception, compassion, and strength that didn't exist in the same way before.

This doesn't mean romanticizing the harm. It means refusing to abandon the you who survived it.

You can say, "I wish that hadn't happened," and also say, "I'm proud of the person I've become through facing it."

You can grieve what you lost and still claim the wisdom and clarity you've gained.

**Healing through Allowance, Not Judgment**

If you've spent years being judged, criticized, or blamed, it can be surprisingly easy to turn those same tools on yourself.

You might catch yourself thinking:

- "I should be over this by now."
- "I'm so stupid for falling for it."
- "If I were really healing, I wouldn't still react this way."

Judgment promises control. It whispers, "If I punish myself enough, I'll make sure this never happens again." But what judgment actually does is freeze you in place. It keeps you cycling through shame instead of moving forward.

Allowance is different.

Allowance simply means you're willing to acknowledge what is – your thoughts, your feelings, your reactions – without making yourself wrong for having them. It doesn't mean you're fine with what happened or that you'll tolerate it again. Allowance is not the same as acceptance.

Allowance sounds like:

- "Of course part of me still misses them. That was a big attachment."
- "Of course I got triggered. This touches old wounds."
- "Of course I'm tired. This has been a lot."

When you meet your experience with allowance instead of judgment, your system can finally start to settle.

Instead of piling shame on top of pain, you offer yourself space. Instead of demanding that you heal on a timeline, you let your process be your process.

This doesn't mean you never challenge your thoughts or behaviors. It means you challenge them from curiosity, not contempt. You might ask, "Is this belief actually kind to me?" or "Does this reaction still serve me?" rather than, "What's wrong with me for feeling this way?"

Energetically, allowance feels softer and more spacious than judgment. Your body may loosen a little. Your breath may deepen. You may notice that when you stop attacking yourself, you have more energy available for actual change.

In the context of gaslighting recovery, allowance is a way of turning off the internalized gaslighter – the part of you that echoes their voice and keeps the story going long after they're gone.

Simply put...

| Allowance | Acceptance | Judgment |
| --- | --- | --- |
| Makes room for your feelings and process. | Can be confused with tolerating what hurt you. | Makes you wrong for how you healed or survived. |
| Sounds like: "Of course this affected me." | Can sound like: "I guess it wasn't that bad." | Sounds like: "I should be over this by now." |
| Honors your reality without forcing a timeline. | May pressure you to normalize or minimize harm. | Keeps shame, self-blame and self-gaslighting alive. |
| Supports healing by creating space and choice. | Can become resignation if it asks you to make peace too. | Blocks healing by turning into proof that something is wrong with you. |

### Choosing to Include Yourself in Your Choices Again

One of the most subtle impacts of gaslighting is how it trains you to disappear from your own choices.

You may have learned to ask:

- "What will keep them calm?"
- "What will make them stay?"
- "What will prove I'm good/loyal/forgiving enough?"

Your decisions became coping strategies for managing someone else's nervous system, image, or approval. Your own needs, desires, and limits were either secondary, or not on the list at all.

Recovery asks a different question: "Where am I in this choice?"

Including yourself in your choices doesn't mean ignoring the impact on others. It means you are also in the equation.

Practically, this might look like:

- Checking in with your body before saying yes: "Do I feel open or tight?"
- Asking, "If I choose this, what will it be like for me in a week? A month? A year?"
- Noticing when you're about to say yes out of fear, obligation, or guilt, and pausing long enough to see if there's another option.

At first, this can feel selfish or wrong, especially if you were praised for self-sacrifice or told that your needs were "too much." You might even hear the old gaslighting voices in your head: "You're making everything about you."

But here's the truth: *you are the one living your life.* You are the one who has to inhabit the outcomes of your choices.

Including yourself is not self-centered. It's sane.

And for many people, that can feel deeply unfamiliar. If you've been taught that centering yourself is selfish, unkind, or dangerous, even the idea of including yourself in your choices can trigger guilt. Maybe you were praised for disappearing into other people's needs, moods, and expectations. Maybe being "good" meant being accommodating, agreeable, or endlessly understanding. But there is a difference between being self-centered and being selfish. Selfishness ignores the reality of others. Being self-centered, in a healthy sense, simply means that you are rooted in yourself while you move through your life. You are not abandoning other people, you are just no longer abandoning you.

When you are creating your life, it makes sense that your life would include you at the center of it. Not as the only person who matters, but as the person whose body, nervous system, values, limits, and desires must be part of the decision-making process. A life built entirely around managing other people's reactions will never feel like home. A life that includes you – your truth, your capacity, your joy, your needs – has the possibility of becoming real, sustainable, and kind. Healing often involves learning that putting yourself back in the center of your choices is not a moral failure. It's how you begin to build a life that actually belongs to you.

You don't have to overhaul every choice overnight. You can start small:

- Choosing to rest when you're tired, even if there are still dishes in the sink.
- Choosing to leave a conversation when your body starts to shut down, even if you worry they'll be upset.
- Choosing to spend time with people who leave you feeling more like yourself, rather than less.

Each time you include yourself, you send a new message to your system: "I matter in my own life." Over time, this becomes the new baseline. You no longer treat your needs and perceptions as negotiable extras. They become central to how you navigate the world.

### End-of-Chapter Exercise: Walking a Nonlinear Path

Use these prompts to gently explore your own recovery process. There is no "right" way to answer. Let whatever comes up be welcome.

1. **Pause.** Take a moment to reflect on the healing

process you've been moving through. In your journal, make a list of the emotions that have appeared along the way – anger, relief, sadness, confusion, hope, numbness, or anything else that has surfaced. As you look at your list, notice how many of these emotions seem to cycle or repeat. Write about what it feels like to consider that this movement may be part of healing itself rather than a sign that you are doing something wrong.

2. **Observe.** Write a letter to the version of you who remained in a gaslighting dynamic longer than you wish you had. Speak to them from the perspective you have now. As you write, reflect on what they did not yet have access to – perhaps support, information, language, tools, or perspective – and how those things are beginning to change your understanding today.

3. **Witness the Pattern.** Notice one place where you have been judging your own process. Perhaps you have thought, "I should be further along," "I shouldn't still think about them," or "I shouldn't still get triggered." In your journal, write down that judgment and then respond to it with compassion. What might it sound like to meet that same place with patience and understanding instead?

4. **Exit the Reaction.** Now look at a choice you are currently facing, whether large or small. Ask yourself, Where am I in this decision? Write down what you want, what you fear, and what might be kind to you in this situation. You don't need to act on the decision right away. The purpose here is simply to see the choice more clearly from your own perspective.

5. **Return to Yourself.** Place a hand somewhere on your body – your heart, chest, or belly – and take a slow breath. In your journal or out loud, say: "My healing doesn't have to be linear to be real. I am allowed to take the time I take. I am allowed to include myself now." Notice any sensations, resistance, or relief that arise. Let whatever you feel be present.

Recovery isn't a straight path out of the fog. It's a series of steps – forward, sideways, and sometimes back – that all count.

***Every moment you choose awareness, allowance, and including yourself, you're moving, whether or not it looks like progress from the outside.***

# Conclusion: Becoming Ungaslightable

You've made it all the way here. That alone says something important about you.

You didn't get to this page by accident. You got here because some part of you refused to keep living in the fog. Some part of you knew that what you were experiencing wasn't "just how it is," and the way you were being treated, or the way you were treating yourself, wasn't the full story of who you are.

Let's finish this together.

**You Are Not Crazy, You're Aware**

If there's one message I want you to carry from this book into the rest of your life, it's this:

*You are not crazy. You're aware.*

Gaslighting depends on you believing that your awareness is the problem. It works by taking your sensitivity, your perception, your deep capacity to feel and notice, and turning those very gifts against you.

"You're too sensitive."
"You're overreacting."
"You're imagining things."
"You're twisting my words."

But look at what actually brought you here.

It wasn't your *madness*, it was your *awareness*.

It was the knot in your stomach when someone's apology didn't match their actions. It was the way your body tightened every time you were told a story that didn't line up with what you saw. It was the quiet discomfort you felt in environments where everyone else seemed fine but you felt something was off.

That's not *craziness*. That's *awareness*.

Throughout this book, you've practiced naming what you perceive, tracking how your body responds, and honoring your internal compass saying, "That's not quite right" even when others denied it. That's you strengthening the muscles that gaslighting tried to atrophy.

You might still have days of doubt. You might still hear

old voices echo in your mind. That's okay. Doubt doesn't erase your awareness, it just means you're human and you're untangling from a system that taught you to distrust yourself.

Every time you say, "I know what I know," even quietly, even just to yourself, you are shutting off another valve in the gas line.

**Your Life Isn't a Tragedy**

Gaslighting experiences can be devastating. There's no way around that. They can impact your relationships, your work, your health, your finances, and your sense of who you are. They can leave you grieving years, that you wish had gone differently.

You are not a cautionary tale. You are not the sum total of what was done to you.

Your story includes pain, confusion, and loss, but it also includes survival, insight, and an extraordinary capacity to see what others miss. It includes the moment you first questioned the narrative. It includes every time you chose to listen to the tiny, stubborn voice inside that said, "Something here doesn't make sense."

If you only look at your life through the lens of "What they did to me," you'll miss the bigger picture: who you became *in spite of it*, who you're becoming now, and who you are going to be.

You've learned to read energy as well as words. You've learned what love isn't. You've learned the difference between apology and manipulation, between influence and control, between discomfort that leads to growth and discomfort that erases you. *None of that justifies the harm.*

Your life is in motion. You are in the middle of the story, not at the end of it.

Every boundary you set, every moment you choose rest over self-attack, every time you believe your body instead of someone else's spin, that's you writing new chapters. That's you shifting from surviving the story to authoring it.

So when the grief comes (*and it will*), let it. When regret shows up, you can acknowledge it: "Of course I wish things had been different." And then you can add, "But I refuse to let this be the only thing my life is about."

You get to have joy. You get to have beauty. You get to have boring, peaceful days where no one is demanding that you explain yourself. You get to create a reality where your nervous system doesn't have to be on trial. ***You get to be you.***

Your life isn't a tragedy. It's a powerful, imperfect, ongoing creation. And you are the one creating it. Now, what can you choose?

**You Don't Have to Fix Them to Free Yourself**

Here's where many people get stuck:

"I understand what happened. I see the patterns, but I can't rest until they understand too."

If that's you, take a breath. You don't have to fix them to free yourself.

You don't have to get a confession, a perfect apology, or a shared version of history. You don't need them to admit they gaslit you. You don't need them to wake up, get therapy, or finally become the person they pretended to be in the beginning.

Would it be nice if some of those things happened? Of course.

Is your freedom dependent on them? No, because people in these types of relationship rarely see faults in themselves.

A big part of what helps people heal is realizing that

gaslighting is often not actually personal, even though it lands in deeply personal ways. That does not make it less harmful, and it does not excuse the behavior. But in many gaslighting dynamics, the other person is not responding to the truth of who you are – they are reacting to the threat your reality creates for their internal stability.

Your clarity, your memory, your boundary, your independence, or your refusal to agree with their version of events can activate shame, defensiveness, or a loss of control in someone who is psychologically organized around protecting a fragile self-image.

This is where the fragile ego of a narcissistic or chronically gaslighting person becomes relevant. Beneath the certainty, blame, superiority, or distortion is often a very limited capacity to tolerate being wrong, exposed, disappointed, or emotionally accountable. Rather than metabolizing those feelings internally, they defend against them by projecting, rewriting, minimizing, or attacking.

In other words, the gaslighting often functions as a psychological defense: a way to regulate their own ego by destabilizing yours. That is why trying to get a clear, mutual reckoning from them so often leads nowhere. The system was never built for reflection. It was built to protect their self-concept at your expense. And once you understand that, you can stop measuring your freedom by their ability to tell the truth about themselves.

Your freedom lives in *your choices*, not in *their changes.*

It lives in the moment you stop arguing with a story that was never written in good faith.

It lives in the decision to walk out of the courtroom where you were always going to be found guilty.

It lives in the quiet clarity of, "I see what this is, and I am no longer available to play this role."

You can leave a conversation, a dynamic, an entire relationship without ever getting a satisfying emotional "ending." And you never have to justify anything you do or choose. That unfinished feeling you keep trying to resolve with them? That's actually your relationship with you asking for attention.

So instead of, "What do they need to do so I can heal?" you might start asking:

- "What do I need to acknowledge so I can heal?"
- "What boundaries will support my nervous

system now?"

- "How can I honor the part of me that stayed, and the part of me that finally chose to leave?"

Fixing them keeps your energy oriented around their choices. Freeing yourself brings your energy back home.

You may still hope they change. You may still care about them. You may even choose, in some cases, to stay in partial contact. But you're no longer waiting for their transformation as the condition for your own.

You are allowed to move forward while they stay the same.

You are allowed to build a life that makes their version of you irrelevant.

You are allowed to be done, even if they never understand why.

**A Final Word**

You've walked through a lot in these pages: definitions and distinctions, stories and tactics, nervous system patterns and energetic awareness, tools and practices, boundaries and new possibilities.

Maybe you don't feel "ungaslightable" yet. That's okay.

This isn't a certification you pass. It's a relationship you build with your own knowing, your own body, your own presence. For once in your life, *it's all about you.*

So as you close this book, I'd love to leave you with a few invitations:

1. **Keep listening to you.** When something feels off, believe yourself enough to get curious. Your discomfort is information, not proof that you're broken.

2. **Let your healing be messy.** Spirals are allowed. Setbacks are allowed. Missing them is allowed. You don't have to perform a perfect recovery to deserve peace.

3. **Choose people and spaces that make room for you.** Your reality, your boundaries, your joy all deserve to exist in relationships, not just in your journal.

4. **Remember that you are the source of your own reality.** Gaslighting tried to convince you otherwise. Guess what. It failed becuase you're here.

The gas will still exist in the world. There will still be people and systems invested in distortion, control, and denial. But you don't have to keep supplying the fuel.

You can notice the lie, feel the impact, and then choose something else.

You can build a life where your reality is not up for debate.

You can surround yourself with people who don't need you confused to feel powerful.

You can wake up each day a little more rooted in the quiet, radical truth:

***You are not crazy. You're aware.***
***You are not broken. You're whole.***
***And you never have to abandon yourself again.***

# RESOURCES

# P.O.W.E.R.

*Feel free to rip this page out and carry it with you. Use this when you feel confused, pressured, or like you're losing yourself. The goal is not to win the moment. The goal is to come back to you.*

**P – Pause**

Stop. Don't react. Don't explain. Don't defend. Just breathe.

**O – Observe**

What just changed? Your body, your emotions, the conversation. Notice without judging.

**W – Witness the Pattern**

Have you felt this before? Do you suddenly feel "wrong"? Are you trying to fix, prove, or explain yourself? Does this feel familiar? This may not be about this moment.

**E – Exit the Reaction**

You do not have to engage. You don't need to prove your reality. You don't need to win the conversation. You don't need to respond right now. Silence is an option.

**R – Return to Yourself**

Come back to what you know. What did you actually see or hear? What feels true for you? If no one disagreed with you, what would you believe? Trust that.

# Quick Reference: Charts

**Figure 1: Differences between manipulation and gaslighting.**

| Manipulation | Gaslighting |
|---|---|
| Goal: influence your behavior or choice | Goal: control your perception of reality |
| Methods: guilt, pressure, persuasion, emotional leverage | Methods: denial, rewriting events, questioning your memory or sanity |
| Reaction: giving in to avoid conflict (if you notice at all). | Reaction: questioning your memory and perception, justifying and defending your choices. |
| Your reality is usually still acknowledged and you still trust you. | Your reality is invalidated or erased and you doubt yourself. |

**Figure 2: Gaslighting effects in different environments**

| Context | Gaslighting Phrase | Hidden Message | Likely Effect |
|---|---|---|---|
| **Codependent Relationship** | "You wouldn't survive without my help." | *You are incapable without me.* | Dependency and reduced self-confidence. |
| **Work Environment** | "Everyone else understands this – why don't you?" | *You're the problem.* | Isolation and insecurity about competence. |
| **Spiritual Circles** | "Your ego is getting in the way of your growth." | *Your concerns are invalid.* | Feeling ashamed for questioning authority. |
| **Society/ Cultural Narratives** | "That didn't happen the way you think it did." | *Your experience of events is unreliable.* | Collective confusion about reality. |

**Figure 3: Difference between gaslighting relationships and conscious relationships**

| Gaslighting | Conscious Relationship |
|---|---|
| Your reality is questioned. | Your reality is respected. |
| Conflict creates confusion. | Conflict can lead to repair. |
| You feel pressure to prove yourself. | You can express yourself clearly. |
| Boundaries are treated as a threat. | Boundaries are part of care. |
| You leave feeling smaller. | You leave feeling more like yourself. |
| Connection feels conditional. | Connection makes room for you. |

**Figure 4: Difference between allowance, acceptance and judgment**

| Allowance | Acceptance | Judgment |
|---|---|---|
| Makes room for your feelings and process. | Can be confused with tolerating what hurt you. | Makes you wrong for how you healed or survived. |
| Sounds like: "Of course this affected me." | Can sound like: "I guess it wasn't that bad." | Sounds like: "I should be over this by now." |
| Honors your reality without forcing a timeline. | May pressure you to normalize or minimize harm. | Keeps shame, self-blame and self-gaslighting alive. |
| Supports healing by creating space and choice. | Can become resignation if it asks you to make peace too. | Blocks healing by turning into proof that something is wrong with you. |

# Discussion Guide

*This guide is designed for book clubs, support circles, workshops, and trusted conversations. Use it to create more room for awareness, self-trust, and honest reflection.*

This book is not meant to be something you simply read and leave behind. It is a tool to help you recognize yourself, reflect on your experiences, and, when it feels helpful, talk them through with others who are also reclaiming their reality.

If you're reading this book in a discussion group, book club, support circle, workshop, or even with one trusted friend, let this chapter be a guide, not a rulebook. The goal is not to diagnose other people or prove who had it worse. The goal is awareness, and creating more room for choice and self-trust.

**Before You Begin**

- Speak from your own experience. Try using "I" statements rather than generalizations.
- Don't force disclosure. People should be free to pass, listen quietly, or share only what they wish.

- Resist the urge to fix. Often the greatest contribution is simply listening without response.
- Let different experiences exist. Not everyone's gaslighting experience will look the same.
- Come back to the body. If discussion gets intense: pause, breathe, and feel your feet on the floor.

**Suggested Ways to Use This Guide**

- Discuss one chapter at a time.
- Choose 2 – 3 questions per meeting rather than trying to answer everything.
- Journal privately before sharing aloud.
- Use the P.O.W.E.R. process if discussion becomes emotionally overwhelming.
- Close each meeting by naming one thing you are taking with you.

**Facilitator Notes**

- Normalize pauses. Silence is not failure. Sometimes people are processing deeply.
- Watch for overwhelm. If someone becomes flooded, invite grounding rather than more disclosure.
- Do not make the group a courtroom. The point is not to prove whose interpretation is right.

- Let awareness unfold. Sometimes the most powerful shift is simply someone realizing, "I've never had words for this before."

## General Discussion Questions for the Whole Book

1. What part of this book made you feel most seen or validated?
2. What definitions, examples, or distinctions changed the way you understand gaslighting?
3. Where did you notice yourself confusing gaslighting with manipulation, conflict, or misunderstanding before reading this?
4. What part of the book felt hardest to read? What part felt most freeing?
5. How has this book changed the way you think about awareness, self-trust, and choice?
6. What patterns did you begin to recognize in your own life that you had not fully named before?
7. What is one idea from the book that you want to keep returning to?

## Discussion Questions by Theme

### *Reality and Self-Trust*

- What does it mean to you to "believe what you

see"?

- Where in your life have you been taught to distrust your own awareness?
- What helps rebuild self-trust after gaslighting?

### *The Energetic Side of Gaslighting*

- What stood out to you about the idea that gaslighting is not only emotional or mental, but also energetic?
- Have you ever felt something was *off* before you could explain it logically?
- How do you recognize that kind of awareness in your body now?

### *The Seductive Cycle of Emotional Control*

- Which tactic in Chapter 4 stood out most strongly for you?
- What makes those tactics easy to miss at first?
- How does the cycle create confusion and attachment at the same time?

### *Self-Gaslighting*

- Which inner phrases feel familiar to you?
- What did you notice in yourself while reading the chapter on self-gaslighting?
- What does it look like to begin choosing what's

true for you again?

### *Boundaries and Choice*

- What does "boundaries without defense" mean to you?
- How did the book change your understanding of boundaries?
- Where are you still trying to win instead of simply choosing?

### *Recovery and Allowance*

- What does it mean that recovery is not linear?
- Where do you most judge your own recovery?
- What would allowance look like in place of that judgment?

### *Conscious Relationships*

- What is the difference between a gaslighting relationship and a conscious relationship?
- What do you now know you deserve?
- Where do you still see a gap between what you deserve and what you accept?

## Chapter-by-Chapter Discussion Prompts

### *Introduction*

- What did the phrase "You are not crazy – you're aware" bring up for you?

- What do you think this book is inviting you to reclaim?

***Chapter 1: What Is Gaslighting, Really?***

- What distinction between manipulation and gaslighting felt most important?
- Where have you experienced control disguised as care, logic, or certainty?

***Chapter 2: Who Gaslights and Why?***

- What stood out to you about the different types of gaslighting personalities and systems?
- What does discernment mean to you after reading this chapter?

***Chapter 3: The Gas Supply: You***

- What does it mean that the gaslighter needs your energy?
- Where do you notice yourself still supplying gas through reaction, explanation, or self-doubt?

***Chapter 4: The Seductive Cycle of Emotional Control***

- Which part of the cycle was easiest to recognize in your own life?
- What does this chapter teach about intensity versus love?

*Chapter 5: Self-Gaslighting*

- What is the difference between being gaslit by others and gaslighting yourself?
- How did the concept of echoism land for you?

*Chapter 6: Gaslighting in the Wild*

- How does gaslighting change when it becomes collective or institutional?
- How do you stay connected to your own reality in environments like that?

*Chapter 7: Awareness Is the Antidote*

- What does presence do that reaction cannot?
- How do you notice the "hooks" before they land?

*Chapter 8: Shifting from Victim to Source*

- What does being the source of your life mean to you?
- What are some small, self-honoring choices that have mattered in your life?

*Chapter 9: Boundaries without Defense*

- What does it mean to make someone irrelevant without needing to win?
- How do cognitive fog and confusion keep people engaged in the cycle?

*Chapter 10: Shutting Off the Gas, Every Day*

- Which daily practices felt most useful or realistic for you?
- What does happiness as resistance mean to you?

*Chapter 11: Choosing Conscious Relationships*

- How do you know when a relationship makes more room for you, not less?
- What old dynamics are you no longer willing to recreate?

*Chapter 12: Recovery Isn't Linear*

- Which part of recovery do you judge most in yourself?
- What does it mean to include yourself in your choices again?

*Conclusion: Becoming Ungaslightable*

- What felt most empowering in the conclusion?
- What does becoming "ungaslightable" mean to you now?

**Closing Questions for Any Group Meeting**

- What is one thing you are taking with you from this conversation?
- What is one thing you are seeing more clearly now?

- What is one choice you want to make from greater self-trust?
- What would it look like to leave this conversation more "with you" than when you entered it?

### Final Invitation

You do not have to read this book perfectly. You do not have to discuss it perfectly. You do not have to heal in a neat, linear, impressive way.

You only have to stay willing to notice.

To notice what is true.
To notice what isn't yours.
To notice where you leave yourself.
And to notice where you are ready, even now, to return.

That is where real discussion begins. And sometimes, that is where healing does too.

# The Myth of Echo and Narcissus

*The story of Echo and Narcissus comes from Metamorphoses by Ovid published in 8 CE. (Adapted from a public domain translation of Ovid's Metamorphoses-Book III).*

Tiresias, whose fame for prophecy had spread throughout the cities, was consulted by the nymph Liriope about her son. She had borne a child of wondrous beauty, Narcissus, and asked whether he would live to a ripe old age. Tiresias replied, **"If he never comes to know himself."**

The answer seemed strange at the time.

As Narcissus grew, his beauty drew the attention of many, both maidens and youths, but he rejected them all with cold pride.

Among those who saw him was Echo, a mountain nymph. Once she had a voice of her own, but because she had distracted Juno with endless chatter, she was cursed to repeat only the last words spoken to her.

When Echo saw Narcissus wandering in the woods, she fell in love with him. She followed him silently, longing to speak, but unable to begin a conversation.

One day, separated from his companions, Narcissus called out:

"Is anyone here?"

Echo answered softly, "Here."

Encouraged, he said, "Come!"

Echo replied, "Come!" and stepped forward from the trees.

But when she tried to embrace him, Narcissus recoiled.

"Hands off!" he said. "I would rather die than let you possess me."

"Possess me…" Echo repeated, her voice fading as she fled in shame.

From that moment, she hid in caves and forests, wasting away with grief until only her voice remained.

One of the rejected lovers, filled with sorrow, prayed for justice:

"May he love as I have loved – and never obtain what he desires."

The gods heard this prayer.

One day, while hunting, Narcissus came upon a clear pool of water, untouched by man or beast. Tired and thirsty, he bent down to drink and saw his reflection.

He did not know it was himself.

Captivated by the image, he fell deeply in love.

He tried to touch it, but the water rippled and the vision disappeared. When it stilled, the image returned.

He spoke to it:

"Why do you flee from me? Stay, beautiful one! I can see you, but I cannot reach you…"

Gradually, he realized the truth:

**"I am he. I burn with love for my own self."**

But still he could not turn away.

Consumed by longing, he wasted away beside the pool. His body weakened, his color faded, and at last, he died.

When the nymphs came to mourn him, they searched for

his body, but in its place, they found a flower:

White petals surrounding a golden center.

The narcissus.

And somewhere in the hills, Echo still repeats the final words of those who call out...a fading voice, shaped by longing.

# Articles, Books, Movies and Clinical Sources

**Books**

Here is a list of recommended books that I have read and utilized in my own practices. Please note this is not an extensive list and I do not have any sales affiliation with any of these authors.

*Gaslighting: Recognize Manipulative and Emotionally Abusive People – and Break Free by Stephanie Sarkis, Ph.D.* This is the book that started it all for me! After reading this book, I had one of the strongest understandings of how gaslighting appears in different areas and began my exploration into the topic.

*The Covert Passive-Aggressive Narcissist: Recognizing the Traits and Finding Healing After Hidden Emotional and Psychological Abuse by Debbie Mirza* This is one of the most used books for anyone just starting to dissect what narcissism looks like in day-to-day life.

*Should I Stay or Should I Go: Surviving A Relationship with a Narcissist by Ramani Durvasula, Ph.D.* As one of Dr. Durvasula's first books, this book discusses the identifying factors of narcissism and contains information to help you determine whether to stay or leave your relationship.

*"Don't You Know Who I Am?": How to Stay Sane in an Era of Narcissism, Entitlement, and Incivility by Ramani Durvasula, Ph.D.* Another book by Dr. Durvasula exploring the epidemic of narcissism and entitlement that we witness in our lives daily.

*It's Not You: Identifying and Healing from Narcissistic People by Ramani Durvasula, Ph.D.* Being one of Dr. Durvasula's newest books, it explores the recovery side of gaslighting and provides tools you can put into practice.

**Movies**

*Gaslight (1944)*
A movie based on the original playwright which is where the term gaslighting originated.

*Wish (2023)*
This cartoon shows a great example of a powerful leader using the guise of caring through the lense of gasligthing.

*Tangled (2010)*
One of the most common gaslighting fairytale villians is Mother Gothel herself.

*Enough (2002)*

This movie shows a very strong form of gaslighting and it's role in domestive violence. TRIGGER WARNING!

*Encanto (2021)*
In this cartoon you can see a subtle form of gaslighting between Mirabel and Abuela. Great example of gaslighting in families.

*Our Brand is Crisis (2015)*
One of the best films to show the power of the media and politicians in regard to gaslighting.

*The Program (2024)*
This documentary can be triggering to many, but it shows the encompassing nature of flying monkeys as well as institutional gaslighting.

*The Vow (2020)*
This documentary follows the development and escape of individuals in the cult NXIVM. It shows great examples of the communal narcissist and use of spiritual gaslighting. This may be triggering for some audiences.

**Clinical Sources**

*National Domestic Violence Hotline: www.thehotline.org*

The Hotline is a free, confidential, 24/7 resource in the U.S. offering compassionate support and guidance for anyone affected by domestic or relationship abuse – accessible via phone, chat, or text with trained advocates ready to provide crisis intervention, safety planning, and referrals in over 200 languages.

*Wordwide Helpline Database: findahelpline.com*

Find A Helpline, powered by ThroughLine, is a free, global directory that helps users find verified crisis helplines – covering topics like suicide prevention, domestic violence, anxiety, depression, and more – in over 130 countries. It offers access via call, text, and online chat.

*National Suicide Prevention Lifeline: 988lifeline.org/*

The 988 Suicide & Crisis Lifeline (reachable by calling, texting, or chatting at 988 or via 988lifeline.org) offers free, confidential, 24/7 support across the U.S. for mental health, suicidal, or substance-use crises, connecting individuals with trained counselors.

# About the Author

John Wheeler, LPCC-S is a therapist, life coach, and workshop facilitator devoted to helping people reclaim themselves and create lives that actually feel like their own.

With a background that spans education, public service, and mental health, John has worked with people from many walks of life – but a common thread kept showing up: people going against what they know and what they desire in order to maintain relationships, avoid conflict, or meet expectations. Again and again, he witnessed the cost of that disconnection – confusion, anxiety, and a quiet loss of self.

His work is rooted in changing that.

Rather than focusing solely on understanding the behavior of others, John takes a consciousness-based approach that centers around awareness, choice, and self-trust. His work invites people out of reaction, out of defense, out of the need to "figure it all out," and into a space where they can recognize what is true for them and choose from that place.

Through his therapy practice, coaching, and workshops, John combines clinical insight with energetic awareness to create an environment where people often feel something they haven't felt in a long time: space. Space to think. Space to feel. Space to be.

Clients frequently describe leaving his sessions with a greater sense of clarity, a deeper connection to themselves, and a feeling of being relaxed, honored, and understood without judgment.

John's perspective on gaslighting developed through years of study, curiosity, and direct work with clients navigating its effects. While much of the conversation around gaslighting focuses on identifying the behaviors of others, his work emphasizes something different: awareness as the antidote. When you begin to recognize what you know and trust it, you are no longer at the effect of someone else's version of reality.

At the core of his work is a simple knowing: *your body is an instrument of awareness, and it does not lie.* The more you learn to listen to it, the easier it becomes to discern truth from distortion, and to choose from a place of clarity rather than fear or doubt.

John does not approach this work from a place of fighting, fixing, or labeling. He does not see people as broken or as victims. Instead, he meets people where they are, honors their experiences, and supports them in reconnecting with the part of themselves that has always been.

If there is one thing he hopes you take with you, it's this:

*You are not alone.*
*You are not crazy.*
*And what you know is still yours.*

This book, and John's work, are here as resources for you. Not to tell you *who to be*, but to support you in discovering *who you already are*, and in creating whatever future you truly desire.

***www.john-wheeler.com***

# Continue the Conversation

If something in this book resonated with you, let's continue the conversation.

John offers spaces where you can explore this work more deeply—whether that's through private sessions, group workshops, or ongoing programs designed to support you in reconnecting with yourself and choosing your life with greater clarity and ease.

If you'd like to continue in a more ongoing way, you're also invited to explore ***Beyond Gaslighting***, a membership created for deeper conversation, reflection, and support around the themes in this book.

**You can learn more, explore current offerings, join the membership or book a 1:1 with John at:**

***shutoffthegas.com***

***Wherever you are in your process, you are welcome here.***

www.ingramcontent.com/pod-product-compliance
Lightning Source LLC
La Vergne TN
LVHW090936080826
845145LV00003B/766

* 9 7 8 1 6 3 4 9 3 7 6 7 2 *

# Continue the Conversation

If something in this book resonated with you, let's continue the conversation.

John offers spaces where you can explore this work more deeply—whether that's through private sessions, group workshops, or ongoing programs designed to support you in reconnecting with yourself and choosing your life with greater clarity and ease.

If you'd like to continue in a more ongoing way, you're also invited to explore ***Beyond Gaslighting***, a membership created for deeper conversation, reflection, and support around the themes in this book.

**You can learn more, explore current offerings, join the membership or book a 1:1 with John at:**

***shutoffthegas.com***

***Wherever you are in your process, you are welcome here.***

www.ingramcontent.com/pod-product-compliance
Lightning Source LLC
LaVergne TN
LVHW090936080826
845145LV00003B/766

* 9 7 8 1 6 3 4 9 3 7 6 7 2 *